From Good Schools to
GREAT
SCHOOLS

In memory of our good friends Jim Hilton and Larry E. Frase

From Good Schools to
GREAT SCHOOLS

What Their Principals Do Well

Susan Penny Gray
William A. Streshly

Foreword by Marge Hobbs

A JOINT PUBLICATION

CORWIN PRESS
A SAGE Company
Thousand Oaks, CA 91320

NAESP

Artwork by Dr. Chyll at Chyll Productions

For information:

Corwin Press
A SAGE Company
2455 Teller Road
Thousand Oaks, California 91320
www.corwinpress.com

SAGE India Pvt. Ltd.
B 1/I 1 Mohan Cooperative Industrial Area
Sage Publications Asia-Pacific Pte. Ltd.
Mathura Road, New Delhi 110 044
India

SAGE Ltd.
1 Oliver's Yard
55 City Road
London EC1Y 1SP
United Kingdom

SAGE Asia-Pacific Pte. Ltd.
33 Pekin Street #02–01
Far East Square
Singapore 048763

Printed in the United States of America

Library of Congress Cataloging-in-Publication Data

Gray, Susan Penny.
From good schools to great schools: What their principals do well/Susan Penny Gray, William A. Streshly.
    p. cm.
Includes bibliographical references and index.
ISBN 978-1-4129-4898-2 (cloth)
ISBN 978-1-4129-4899-9 (pbk.)
    1. School principals—United States. 2. Educational leadership—United States. 3. School management and administration—United States. I. Streshly, William A. II. Title.

LB2831.92.G73 2008
371.2'011—dc22   2007022028

This book is printed on acid-free paper.

08   09   10   11   10   9   8   7   6   5   4   3

Acquisitions Editor:	Elizabeth Brenkus
Editorial Assistants:	Ena Rosen and Desirée Enayati
Production Editor:	Melanie Birdsall
Copy Editor:	Alison Hope
Typesetter:	C&M Digitals (P) Ltd.
Proofreader:	Gail Fay
Indexer:	Sylvia Coates
Cover Designer:	Rose Storey
Graphic Designer:	Lisa Miller

Contents

List of Figures
and Tables

Foreword

A competitive world has two possibilities for you: you can lose or, if you want to win, you can change.

—Lester Thurow, former dean of the
MIT Sloan School of Management (1938)

When I first learned of the book *Good to Great: Why Some Companies Make the Leap . . . and Others Don't*, by Jim Collins (2001), I wondered how schools and their leaders could use his research to improve the leadership in our public school system. The authors of this book have studied this question by looking closely at a sample of our very best school principals and comparing their behavior and characteristics with Collins' research. What they learned was both surprising and challenging.

As members of the faculty at San Diego State University in Southern California, Susan Penny Gray and William A. Streshly prepare school administrators. They present in this volume evidence that supports a new paradigm for apprenticing school administrators—one that differs from the traditional model of unresearched best practices and standards. The book represents a research-based glimpse into research-based best practices. Grounding the concepts in a research format similar to the one Jim Collins used, the authors have made it their business to become informed about the best ideas and theories of leadership in schools. In this researched model, school site leaders can learn to look closely at their leadership through the experiences of super-star models and reflect on their own behaviors to move schools toward a more excellent school experience for their students. School leaders can use this book to inspire activities that transform their schools and reframe their professional behaviors.

Gray and Streshly maintain that the authors of the Interstate School Leaders Licensure Consortium standards have not gathered sufficient empirical evidence to support their standards, and that the standards too often amount to little more than craft knowledge. This is disturbing to those of us involved with professional development, since the standards being widely adopted by states across the country are based at least in part on that consortium's standards. In using the Collins research model, the authors suggest a new paradigm for school leadership training. They observed some commonalities of leadership with the CEOs Collins studied, as well as an additional concept—the ability to work well with groups.

When my youngest daughter, Alysia, became an administrator last year, she observed that none of the classes she had taken during her administrative credential program was helpful in her planning of what to do at her assigned "failing" middle school. In the jargon of educational administration leadership, she was experiencing a dichotomy between theory and practice. This book will help support my daughter with the critical decisions in her commitment to educating all students at her school, and, as Collins writes, to care enough about the company (students/school/faculty) to endure the pain of "Level 5 decisions." She and I are convinced that, without school leadership knowledge and commitment at Level 5, our national goals of equal access to rigorous content for all students will not be realized.

We know from Collins' research on leadership that there is a gap between the Level 4 and the Level 5 of the five-level hierarchy of leadership ability. Gray and Streshly found the difference between Level 4 and

Level 5 to be the maintenance of gains over a sustained period. This major shift from today's view of excellence is a key difference that is often over-looked and nearly neglected in society's rush to judge schools from the current high-stakes testing frenzy.

"What can I do to make a difference and bring my school to excel-lence?" Do you want to know what to give to that new or experienced principal that will answer that question? The authors have given us insights through conversations with truly great principals so that we may model them and improve our own operations. Using the behaviors of Level 5, super-star principals will support the development of great edu-cational leaders who are able to engage in long-term leadership of schools that are effective for all students and faculty. This book is a valuable preservice book for administrators, as well as a book to be read by all site leaders who are ready to meet the challenge of a school for all students.

—Marge Hobbs, EdD
Director
North County Professional Development Federation
San Diego County, California

Preface

It ain't what you don't know that gets you into trouble. It's what you know for sure that just ain't so.

—Mark Twain (Samuel L. Clemens), author (1835–1910)

The purpose of this book is to explore the leadership characteristics of principals who have enabled their schools to make the leap from good student performance to great student performance. Our intended audience is practicing and aspiring school principals, as well as those responsible for the design and delivery of principal preparation programs.

Inspired by Jim Collins' research on outstanding private sector CEOs as reported in his book *Good to Great* (2001), we embarked on a similar investigation of the qualities of outstanding principals. We compared our findings with Collins' *Good to Great* to see what we could learn from this prominent private sector research. What we learned should help every educator who seeks excellence in school leadership.

As social institutions go, large public schools organized in political hierarchies are fairly new phenomena. The modern-day school principal is also relatively new. These days, buffeted by political storms, the position is changing rapidly. This may be one reason we do not have a lot of empirical data describing what the very best of these leaders do. This state of affairs was unsettling to us as we contemplated redesigning our principal preparation program at San Diego State University. More than a decade earlier, we had participated in the Danforth Foundation's principal preparation network, and as a result had incorporated several effective instructional approaches in our preparation program. Moreover, our department was familiar with the Interstate School Leaders Licensure Consortium (ISLLC) standards and the California version of those standards. Nevertheless, we continued to be bothered by the dearth of research supporting the content of the standards, especially since these standards would soon shape our principal preparation program.

At the same time, we were intrigued by the research on CEOs of very successful companies on which Collins' (2001) bestselling book reports. We wondered if the behaviors and characteristics of our great business leaders that Collins described in this book might also be found among the best of our school principals. Beginning in 2003 and for the next two years, we embarked on a project to find out.

THE PURPOSE OF THE BOOK

The purpose of this book is to share what we learned about the behaviors and characteristics of a group of highly successful, or super-star, school principals. The book is intended for practicing principals, aspiring principals, and their supervisors, as well as for faculty in administrator preparation programs and others interested in the effective leadership of our schools.

While we were conducting our research, we were struck by the idea that the behaviors and characteristics of these stars could be learned. In other words, we could equip most of our administrative candidates with interpersonal skills and approaches to human problems that could help them succeed in doing what they set out to do. At the same time, we are also realistic about the weight of our findings. This was a small study, and although the findings raise important questions, they must be viewed as clues, not as conclusions. We were convinced, however, that sharing these clues with our colleagues was extremely important for two powerful reasons: the behaviors of the principals we studied tended to match the CEOs studied by Collins, and—probably most important—the behaviors of the principals we studied were linked directly to student achievement.

ISLLC STANDARDS

Some of the ISLLC standards are supported by sound empirical evidence. Much of it, however, is craft knowledge or best practices. The origin of this craft knowledge often harkens back to brainstorming sessions with prominent educators and experts who then validate the resulting standards. This means they are read and judged to be accurate by a large number of the same sort of experts who developed them to begin with. In a sharp criticism of the process, Fenwick English (2005) recounted that the Educational Testing Service used 14 subject-matter experts to conduct a job analysis. This resulted in statements about the responsibilities and knowledge areas needed by beginning school administrators. These statements were then mailed to more than 10,000 principals who either agreed or disagreed with the statements. English averred that the exercise is a validation exercise: "It is not a measure of the truthfulness of the responsibilities or knowledge areas per se" (p. 5).

To be clear, the ISLLC standards accomplished what they were supposed to accomplish. They are an example of the best we can come up with, given our present knowledge base. As a result of our discomfort with the dearth of hard data to support these standards, we became convinced not only that more research is needed, but also that another approach is vital.

GOOD TO GREAT

For this reason, our interest was aroused by Collins' (2001) work. He began by identifying great companies and asking, "Why?" This approach was similar to what Peters and Waterman ([1982] 2004) did in the 1980s when they investigated the leadership practices of the top companies of that day. The idea in both cases was to examine great operations and determine why they were great.

EXAMINING "GREAT" PRINCIPALS

As we started our research, we became convinced that we could use the same approach Collins used in order to gain insight into the characteristics and behaviors of our very best principals. What ensued was a qualitative examination of six highly successful principals. We wanted to know more about principals who make their schools champions.

TRADITIONAL PRINCIPAL PREPARATION QUESTIONED

We had good reason to wonder about what makes a great school administrator. Our program at San Diego State University had all the regular features—all supported by the conventional wisdom of the craft. Part of the rationale for licensure is to protect the public, and requiring school administrators to be educated in school law would certainly seem to fit this criterion. And how about curriculum management and school finance? Or leadership? All, according to conventional wisdom or craft speculation, should be part of the preservice training in a solid school administrator preparation program.

We were reminded of the experience of a young superintendent we know who was in the first year of his first superintendency. The county superintendent usually called on the local district superintendents to screen papers for superintendent openings in the county. This young superintendent was asked to serve on the paper-screening committee for a school district superintendency along with two other prominent superintendents—one of whom had been honored recently as superintendent of the year by the American Association of School Administrators. The conversation began with the usual question, "What qualifications are we looking for in a superintendent for this school district?" The young superintendent replied with conviction, "I think he or she should have principal experience."

Years later, the young superintendent recalled he was embarrassed to learn that neither of the successful superintendents he was meeting with that day had been principals. His belief in the necessity of principal experience was based on craft speculation. There was some commonsense support for the notion, but no empirical evidence. We believe that most of what we teach is important, but is it critical in order to prepare great school administrators?

Our research has led us to suspect that highly successful principals possess certain characteristics and behave in specific ways that cause their schools to be very successful. However, our research, like the recent research of Collins (2001) and of Peters and Waterman 19 years before ([1982] 2004), only provides strong inference—not irrefutable truth. Collins studied only 11 companies; Peters and Waterman, 75 companies. Moreover, we tend to believe in naturals: we believe that a few people are endowed with propensities that they are able to develop without a preparation program. Thus, conclusive proof is elusive. We need much more research of the kind Jim Collins has done.

Chapters 1 through 10 attempt to answer the question, "We know what to do, so why do we fail?" We look deeply in this book at specific qualities of the highly successful school principal. The bulk of this book is dedicated to looking at each of the leadership qualities as exhibited by principals whose schools have been very successful in increasing student achievement—regardless of the many barriers the principals have encountered.

In Chapter 11, we consider the commonalities and differences between school principals and business leaders. In addition to a discussion of the disparities, we look at observable leadership attributes universally applied to both public schools and the private sector.

Finally, Chapter 12 provides insights into the potential of people to become successful school leaders. We make a case for a new paradigm for administrative preparation programs that will do more to promote success for school leaders in the work of twenty-first-century schools.

AN INTIMATE LOOK AT SUPER-STAR PRINCIPALS

We invite you to explore with us how Collins' research in the private sector might apply to schools. More than that, we invite you to see how the in-depth discussion of the interviews with each of the highly successful principals gives you a priceless intimate acquaintance with the hearts and minds of star-quality school leaders. You will discover, as we discovered, that these powerful people represent a wide range of personalities, and at the same time exhibit a solid core of leadership qualities and characteristics that coalesce to create startling success in their schools. You will see through the eyes of these leaders in the trenches, and you will experience, through their words, what it takes to produce great schools.

At the end of each chapter, we have posed some key questions about the leadership principles discussed in the chapter. We encourage you to reflect on these questions as they apply to your own professional growth. In addition, we offer suggestions to principals who are working to adapt the text for their own use.

Acknowledgments

This book began as a research study. As such, we owe a great debt to the late Larry Frase of San Diego State University and Bruce Matsui and Charles Kerchner of Claremont Graduate University for their guidance in the planning, implementation, and analysis of the study. In addition, our thanks go to the faculty of the Educational Leadership Department of San Diego State University for sharing their words of wisdom with us, and serving as a valuable resource for information about the current status of school administrator preparation.

The process of turning a research study into a book manuscript takes time—not only for the hours of rewriting and reorganization, but also for the change in mind-set from academic to professional. We acknowledge the assistance Kathy Juline gave us in editing the book and commenting on the voice and flow of the story we told. A special "thank you" goes to Dr. Chyll, who drew the cartoons for this book.

This book and the study it describes would not have been possible without the participation of the 11 principals of the original study. We appreciate their candor and thoughtfulness that led to the insights in this book.

Finally, we would like to thank our respective families for their emotional and intellectual support throughout the development of this book. When we needed feeding, they fed us. When we asked to be left to our work, they shut the door. When we requested an audience to try our ideas out on, they were in the front row.

PUBLISHER'S ACKNOWLEDGMENTS

Corwin Press gratefully acknowledges the contributions of the following individuals:

Brenda Dean, Assistant Superintendent
    for Curriculum and Instruction
Hamblen County Department of Education
Morristown, TN

Mary Lynne Derrington, Professor
Western Washington University
Bellingham, WA

Joen Hendricks-Painter
Educational Consultant
Yuma, AZ

Allison Hoewisch, Associate Professor
St. Norbert College
De Pere, WI

Mary Johnstone, Principal
Rabbit Creek Elementary School
Anchorage, AK

John Pieper, Fifth-Grade Teacher
Webster Stanley Elementary School
Oshkosh, WI

Ted Zigler, Professor
University of Cincinnati
Cincinnati, OH

About the Authors

 **Susan Penny Gray, PhD,** has been an educator for more than 40 years in Indiana and California, including 15 years as Director of Curriculum Services for the San Marcos Unified School District in San Marcos, California, and seven years as a member of the Educational Leadership faculty at San Diego State University (SDSU). During her tenure as Director of Curriculum Services, she was responsible for the development, implementation, and maintenance of exemplary programs in reading and language arts, mathematics, history and social science, and science for Grades K–12; these programs have been recognized throughout California. She was also responsible for effective teacher and principal support strategies that, during the years under her direction, evolved into a powerful system of coaches and facilitators of staff development. Dr. Gray has "walked the talk" in helping principals become truly effective instructional leaders. Her insights give down-to-earth, practical meaning to the research discussed in this book.

Dr. Gray serves on the SDSU Educational Administration Preparation Programs Advisory Committee. In her capacity on this committee and as a current member of the faculty of the Educational Leadership Department in the School of Education at SDSU, she has assisted in implementing changes in that school's administration preparation program. She has designed and currently teaches an administrative course on instructional improvement through evaluation and supervision. In this course, students participate in a walk-through supervision practicum, formal evaluation exercises, and the design of teacher and administrator evaluation systems. In addition, Dr. Gray teaches and coordinates the advanced administrator credentialing program at SDSU and supervises the fieldwork for administrative credential candidates at all levels.

In addition to her involvement with the faculty of Educational Leadership at SDSU, Dr. Gray serves as an officer on the board of directors of California Curriculum Management Systems, Inc. She is certified to train administrators and teachers in conducting walk-throughs to support higher student achievement, and has implemented this training in several states across the country. She has also served as an external evaluator of schools and is a certified School Assistance and Intervention Team Leader for the State of California. She received curriculum management audit training from the California Curriculum Management Audit Center in Burlingame, California, in 1998. Since then, she has served on school district audits in California, Washington, Texas, Ohio, Arizona, Maryland, New York, Virginia, and Pennsylvania. She has also served on academic achievement teams conducting comprehensive on-site assessments of the educational operations of school and community college districts in California.

Dr. Gray earned her undergraduate degree from the University of California, Santa Barbara, and her master's degree from SDSU. In 2005, she received a doctoral degree in educational leadership through the Claremont Graduate University/SDSU Joint Doctoral Program.

 **William A. Streshly, PhD,** is Emeritus Professor of Educational Leadership in the College of Education at San Diego State University (SDSU). Prior to coming to SDSU in 1990, Dr. Streshly spent 25 years in public school administration, including five years as principal of a large suburban high school and 15 years as superintendent of several California school districts that varied in size from 2,500 to 25,000 students.

In addition to his numerous publications in professional journals, Dr. Streshly is author or coauthor of four practical books for school leaders: *The Top 10 Myths in Education, Avoiding Legal Hassles* (two editions), *Teacher Unions and Quality Education,* and *Preventing and Managing Teacher Strikes.*

Professor Streshly serves on the board of directors of California Curriculum Management Systems, Inc. He received his curriculum management audit training in 1990 and now serves as a lead auditor. He has audited the instructional operations of more than 40 school districts in 16 states. His intense interest in the role of effective school leadership stems from his own extensive experience, as well as his in-depth observation of the work of hundreds of practicing school principals across the country.

1

We Know What to Do, So Why Do We Fail?

The problem is not that we do not know enough—it is that we do not do what we already know.

—Schmoker (2005, p. 148)

A t seven in the morning, school district superintendents, directors of instruction, professors of educational leadership, and other educational leaders have gathered on the campus of San Diego State University (SDSU) in San Diego, California. The purpose for the meeting is to brainstorm ways that the Educational Leadership Department at SDSU can assist school districts in their efforts to improve student learning. The room is buzzing with friendly exchanges.

A weary-eyed professor at the far end of the table offers a conversation starter: "Much research points to the promise of increased student learning when school leaders and teachers work together as a professional learning community, sharing the vision and collaborating for such important functions as data analysis, lesson study, and curriculum alignment."

At this point, one noticeably uncomfortable younger superintendent asks pointedly, "Well, if we know what needs to be done to get good results, why can't we do it?" Jeffrey Pfeffer and Robert Sutton (2000), in their study of successful private sector companies, described this divide between knowing what needs to be done and doing it as one of the "great mysteries in organizational management: why knowledge of what needs to be done frequently fails to result in action or behavior consistent with that knowledge" (p. 4).

Responses to the superintendent's question from the school leaders in the room immediately focus on the usual barriers to success: the changing student population, inadequate teacher preparation, English language learner difficulties, lack of parent involvement, bureaucratic requirements, union stalemates, insufficient fiscal resources, and unreasonable pressures of the No Child Left Behind Act.

Most in the group nod their heads in agreement with one superintendent who interjects, "But there are schools out there where student achievement is improving in spite of the barriers we are all talking about." He asks pointedly, "How are they able to get past those barriers?"

THE "GOOD TO GREAT" RESEARCH PROJECT

This pivotal question prompted us to seriously rethink just how some schools are able to succeed in the face of seemingly impossible barriers. The research of Jim Collins, reported in his bestselling book *Good to Great: Why Some Companies Make the Leap . . . and Others Don't* (2001), led us to look to the school leader for answers to the puzzle. Collins was asking the same question we are asking—but he was asking the question in the corporate world. His research team of 21 graduate students from the University of Colorado Graduate School of Business spent five years exploring this question. Their research zeroed in on how good companies become great companies, and how they then stay that way. The great companies of the Collins' study faced all the same constraints of similar companies, yet made gains and sustained those gains, while the other companies made few or no gains, and were unable to sustain any gains they did make. The researchers found that the key to these companies' success was their CEOs. They also found that the CEOs of the successful companies exhibited certain specific powerful characteristics and behaviors. Moreover, these characteristics and behaviors were absent in the leaders of the less-successful companies in the study.

As faculty in the Educational Leadership Department at SDSU, we realized that the results of Collins' research about private sector leadership might hold pieces to the puzzle about what constitutes effective school leadership and why some schools blossom and others don't.

At the time, our interest in successful school leadership was being put to a practical test at SDSU, where we were working to redesign educational administration preparation programs to better prepare principals for twenty-first-century school leadership. Suppose our preparation programs were missing the point?

Collins and his research team addressed precisely the question we wanted to explore in public school leadership. In their study, successful leaders were identified by exploring the characteristics of good companies that transitioned to great companies. Eleven companies were studied that made the leap from good results to great results, and then sustained those results. To select these companies, financial analysis was necessary to find companies that showed a pattern of "good" performance punctuated by a transition point, after which these companies shifted to "great" performance. Naturally, the profit-oriented business performance was defined in terms of corporate profit.

The Level 5 Executive

The study looked at what the great companies had in common that distinguished them from a group of similar comparison companies. Factors were found that were common to all great companies but that did not always exist among the comparison companies. A central element of the research findings was the presence of what Collins (2001) termed a "Level 5 Executive" (p. 20). The Level 5 Executive is at the top of a five-level hierarchy of leadership ability that Collins and his research team developed when they identified shared capabilities of the CEOs of all of the *Good to Great* companies in their research.

We were fascinated to learn that Collins' researchers were not specifically looking for leadership as a necessary ingredient for company success. Nevertheless, the information supporting the distinct role of specific leadership characteristics was overwhelming and convincing. Collins' research team debated extensively how to describe the most effective leaders and finally settled on the label "Level 5 Executive" to avoid making them sound weak or meek. These executives did not necessarily move in sequence from Level 1 to Level 5, but the evolution of the Level 5 Executive is cumulative, with these executives embodying the characteristics of all five levels of the hierarchy. Level 5 Executives build enduring greatness through a paradoxical blend of personal humility and professional will.

The insights into leadership found by the Collins study were both surprising and, in some cases, contrary to conventional wisdom. They suggest a different paradigm for leadership training—one that we suspect has implications for producing successful school leaders.

The Level 5 School Executive

Thus, we set out to determine whether the Collins (2001) research could apply to school leaders. Are there identifiable characteristics of successful school principals that can be correlated with long-term educational success? Could the absence of the leadership characteristics Collins found in his study be the reason many school leaders fail to accomplish what they set out to accomplish? Can the characteristics of great executives be taught and learned as part of an administrator preparation program?

To answer these questions, we studied great school principals using a semistructured qualitative interview technique. We replicated the interview questions in Collins' research of successful private sector companies with modifications for public school leadership, then we interviewed a group of principals whose schools moved from good to great in student achievement and stayed there over a period of time. In keeping with Collins' research protocol, we also studied principals selected as a comparison group. The schools of these comparison principals were good, but did not move to great and stay there. The purpose of our interviews was to examine the leadership characteristics and behaviors of highly successful principals and the comparison principals as reflected in their responses. (Note: The protocol used in our study for selection of participants and interview questions may be found in Resources A, B, and C.)

The Ability to Build Relationships

We found that the principals of highly successful schools in our study exhibited the characteristics and behaviors of the Level 5 Executives of Collins' research with one important difference: all of the highly successful principals also demonstrated a strong ability to build relationships among their faculty. The literature on successful schools, combined with our own research focusing on highly successful principals, has persuaded us that the one most critical piece of the successful school puzzle is the presence of a principal with the critical leadership attribute of building relationships. This quality, along with the characteristics of the Level 5 Executive in Collins' research, make up our framework for the highly successful school principal as defined in Figure 1.1.

Figure 1.1 Framework for the Highly Successful Principal

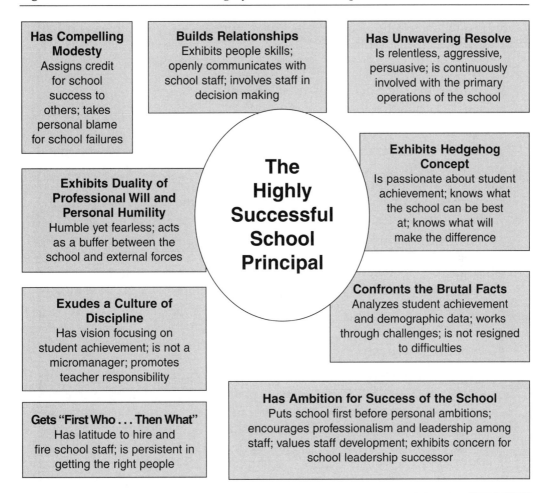

LEADERSHIP CHARACTERISTICS OF LEVEL 5 EXECUTIVES

In Collins' private sector research, every one of the great CEOs in the *Good to Great* companies exhibited certain significant characteristics identifying each of them as a Level 5 Executive.

Duality of Professional Will and Personal Humility

The first of these characteristics was what Collins (2001) termed a "duality of professional will and personal humility" (p. 22). While on the surface the great CEOs in the study seemed quiet and reserved, hidden within each of them was intensity, a dedication to making anything they touched the best it could possibly be. We found this same characteristic among our highly successful principals when we modified Collins' definition of "personal humility." In Chapter 3, we expand on the modification of this characteristic as it pertains to our principals—where it was present and where it was not.

Ambition for the Success of the Company

The second leadership characteristic was "ambition for the success of the company rather than for one's own personal renown" (p. 25). Great private sector leaders want to see the company even more successful in the next generation and are comfortable with the idea that most people won't even know about the efforts they took to ensure future success. Our star principals displayed ambition for the success of the school that rivals the ambition demonstrated by the successful CEOs of the Collins study. In Chapter 5, we demonstrate what we found among all of the highly successful principals, first through the story of energetic Ms. Aspiration, principal of Mission Elementary School. She was able to fuel her own ambition for the success of the school by nurturing the ambitions of each of the faculty to unite in their individual efforts to raise test scores.

Compelling Modesty

A third characteristic identified by Collins' research was "compelling modesty" (p. 27). When things go well, leaders with this trait give credit to others; when things go badly, they accept the blame. During the interviews, the *Good to Great* leaders would talk about the company and the contributions of other executives but would deflect discussion about their own contributions. Prevalent among our highly successful principals was a modesty that on the surface seemed to contradict their ambitions for the success of their school. Mr. Unpretentious of Bay View Elementary, whom we will meet later in this book, serves as a good example of this modesty among our principals. Throughout his interview, he credited the teaching staff for all successes of the school and only when asked about something that was tried but failed did he bring attention to his own contributions— and then only to blame himself for the failure. Conversely, the comparison principals were quick to blame someone other than themselves for failures.

Unwavering Resolve to Do What Must Be Done

It is probably no surprise that the fourth characteristic identified by the researchers was "unwavering resolve" to do what must be done to make the organization successful (p. 30). Leaders with this trait typically are driven with an unshakable need to produce results and to do whatever it takes to make the company great. Ms. Persevere, tireless principal of Mountain High Elementary, is the highly successful principal in Chapter 6 we draw on to demonstrate the unwavering resolve of all of our principals. When teachers are quick to make excuses for not following through with a program or strategy, Ms. Persevere jumps in to do it for them so they have no excuses. Her unwavering resolve to do what needs to be done serves as a model for each of the members of the staff of Mountain High Elementary School.

LEADERSHIP BEHAVIORS OF LEVEL 5 EXECUTIVES

The success of the CEOs of the *Good to Great* companies is not attributed solely to the presence of the key leadership characteristics we have just described. Kirkpatrick and Locke (1991) found that characteristics by themselves tell only part of the story, since there is much more to being an effective leader than the possession of certain characteristics.

> Recent research, using a variety of methods, has made it clear that successful leaders are not like other people. The evidence indicates that there are certain core traits, which contribute to business leaders' success. . . . Leaders do not have to be great men or women by being intellectual geniuses or omniscient prophets to succeed, but they do need to have the "right stuff" and this stuff is not equally present in all people. (pp. 49, 59)

Collins' work expands on the idea of core leadership characteristics working in tandem with leadership behavior. He found a mutual interdependence between the personal characteristics and behaviors of his Level 5 Executive and the remaining findings of his research on companies that transitioned from being good companies to being great companies and sustained this greatness over time. Important leadership behaviors were present in all of the great CEOs; when combined with the leadership attributes, they served to guarantee the successes of these leaders. Of the behaviors Collins describes, we believe four behaviors to be especially relevant to effective school leadership.

"First Who . . . Then What"

The first of these behaviors is what Collins (2001) called "First Who . . . Then What." Great leaders know how to "get the right people on the bus, the wrong people off the bus, and the right people in the right seats" (p. 41). Only then are decisions about which way to go made. In the school business, the great principals learn to manipulate their systems in order to gather the right personnel to do what must be done at their school sites—despite often confronting overwhelming bureaucratic obstacles. In Chapter 7, we visit several of the highly successful principals to examine their almost fanatical strategies for getting the right teachers for their school, eliminating teachers who did not fit with the vision or focus of the school, and only then making decisions about the way to go in moving their schools to greatness. We will visit comparison principals who, as reflected in their interviews, were resigned to the fact that they had no authority to hire and fire.

Confront the Brutal Facts

The second behavior is what Collins recognized as the ability of the great leader to "confront the brutal facts" (p. 65). Great leaders maintain unwavering faith that the company can and will prevail in the end, regardless of the difficulties, and at the same time have the discipline to confront the most brutal facts of the company's current reality. Great leaders do not fool themselves or try to sugarcoat problems. All of our highly successful principals demonstrated this behavior. For instance, Mr. Focus confronts the very real fact that the majority of the student population at his school came to them with poor reading skills. His unwavering resolve and ambition for the success of the school assures him that he and his disciplined staff can do something about it, regardless of the difficulties. On the other hand, as described earlier, the comparison principals we examined in our study simply resigned themselves to the impossibility of what they considered a barrier to a given situation.

The Hedgehog Concept

Collins identified a third behavior that he termed the "hedgehog concept" (p. 94), which he borrowed from the ideas of Isaiah Berlin in his famous essay *The Hedgehog and the Fox* (1993). Berlin divided the world into hedgehogs and foxes, based on an ancient Greek parable: "The fox knows many things, but the hedgehog knows one big thing." Collins (2001) found that the great CEOs "know what their company can do the best, what their economic engine is, and what their passion is all combined into one crystalline concept" (pp. 95–96). In our study of successful principals, we needed to first understand the parameters within which this concept applies to schools, given the differences between schools and business organizations. For school principals, the hedgehog concept consists of knowing what teachers are best at (e.g., skill and determination), determining what drives the educational engine of the school (e.g., increasing time spent teaching reading), and being a fanatic about the school's educational engine. We will consider these parameters in detail in Chapter 9 when we visit Mr. Focus. His interview responses reflect his embrace of the hedgehog concept. He knows that skill and determination of his teachers in teaching students is top notch. He knows that if his students read well, they will perform well, and he is passionate about it.

Culture of Discipline

Collins found that great leaders exemplified a "culture of discipline" made up of "disciplined people, disciplined thought, and disciplined action"

(p. 127) where people understand they have a responsibility, not a job, and they have freedom within the context of that responsibility to take action. This attribute encompasses all three of the preceding behavioral attributes described in this chapter: "First Who . . . Then What," confront the brutal facts, and the hedgehog concept. In Chapter 10, we call on Ms. Discipline who, like all of the highly successful principals and their staffs in our study, exudes a culture of discipline.

TWO BEHAVIORS FROM THE COLLINS STUDY

Two behaviors identified by Collins (2001) but which were not singled out for our study of successful principals are "technology accelerators" and the "flywheel" and the "doom loop."

Technology Accelerators

In the Collins study, the great CEOs thought differently about technology. They avoided technology fads, holding tight to their hedgehog concept. Instead, they used technology as an accelerator toward their economic engine—profit—and were pioneers in technology only when it furthered their hedgehog concept. Collins found that the way in which a company reacts to technology is a good indicator of greatness. We believe this is also true of great school leaders. Mediocre principals take on new technology just for the sake of keeping up with change and trying out something new and interesting. Highly successful principals use technology to accelerate the momentum of what drives their educational engine: student performance. Seldom are they pioneers in new technology because their purpose is different. They are not in the profit-making business; they are in the student performance business. Technology is one resource of many used to arrive at that end. We do not include a separate study of technology accelerators in our examination of highly successful principals because decisions made about technology were reflective, for the most part, of these principals staying the course found in evidence for the hedgehog concept and a culture of discipline.

Flywheel Versus the Doom Loop

This behavior is discussed last for good reason. The transformation from good to great in the private sector comes about by a snowballing process—step by step, action by action, decision by decision—until the company reaches greatness. Collins referred to this process as the "flywheel." All of the characteristics and behaviors discussed thus far are the necessary ingredients that make up the flywheel pattern. This process occurs in the schools of highly successful principals as well. In our interviews with these leaders, when asked what factors contributed to the success of their schools, they would reveal that success wasn't due to a single program or event but instead was a process that evolved over time. Often the media covers the success of a school after it has made its breakthrough, giving the impression that the transformation occurred overnight. In reality, the tranformative process of getting there was probably slow. Collins and his team found a very different pattern in the comparison companies. These companies changed course often, launching into something new and failing to build sustained results. This approach often led comparison companies to bankruptcy, buyouts, mergers, or other disappointing measures. Collins called this occurrence a "doom loop."

Just as in the case of the private sector, when considering successful schools, we believe the flywheel concept is the structural pattern that encompasses "disciplined people, disciplined thought, and disciplined action" and people who are hedgehogs about their focus. In the case of the comparison principals, the doom loop is the pattern that houses all their characteristics and behaviors that keep them from moving forward. Therefore, we decided for our study of highly successful principals not to treat the flywheel versus the doom loop as a distinct set of behaviors. Instead, we considered them as the structural patterns that support all the other important behavioral attributes in our study, especially the hedgehog concept and culture of discipline.

GREAT SCHOOL EXECUTIVES
BUILD RELATIONSHIPS

Using the Collins research methodology, we found the characteristics and behaviors identified by Collins to be useful in characterizing principals of great schools. However, during our research of successful principals, we discovered an additional critical leadership quality—the ability to build relationships. While this ability was not identified as a behavior in Collins' research of successful private sector CEOs, it surfaced prominently during the conversations we had with the highly successful school principals in our study. Building relationships is understandably essential for an environment that embraces collaboration, communication, and professional learning communities in schools. In Chapter 2, we meet Mr. Bond, principal of Field Elementary School. He attributes the success of his school in improving student performance to the evolution of the teachers toward collaboration and communication, and demonstrates his ability to build relationships in helping them do this.

The highly successful principals we interviewed exhibited, to some extent, all the characteristics and pertinent behaviors of the Level 5 Executive of Collins' research, as well as the capacity for building relationships. Some of these principals excel in certain areas more than in others. Each of the principals, to varying degrees, demonstrates all of the attributes.

Similar to the 11 companies of Collins' study, great schools are those that make great improvement in student achievement and sustain that greatness. A surprise in the Collins (2001) study was the finding that Level 5 Executives had common characteristics that were absent in the CEOs of companies he compared to his *Good to Great* companies. We observed similar differences when comparing our great principals with their comparison group counterparts.

To photograph truthfully and effectively is to see beneath the surfaces and record the qualities of nature and humanity which live or are latent in all things.

—Ansel Adams, photographer (1902–1984)

THE SCHOOL PRINCIPALS IN OUR STUDY

In the next nine chapters, a select group of highly successful school principals will be examined for who they are and what they do through the lenses used by Collins in his research of successful CEOs as reported in *Good to Great* (2001). In our research, we identified a comparison group of principals to observe whether certain leadership qualities shared by highly successful principals are different from those of other principals. As we explained earlier, our research was inspired by Jim Collins' research. The difference between the good schools headed by principals in the comparison group and the great schools headed by principals in the highly successful group was whether or not their schools made a leap to success and whether this success was sustained over time.

Although our sample represented principals in a wide variety of school settings, all were from California. However, the qualities we found in them are most certainly qualities found in successful principals elsewhere. We are experienced curriculum management auditors licensed by Curriculum Management Systems, Inc., and have studied principals in widely diverse settings in more than 30 states. In those studies, we were struck by the similarity of the school principal's job from state to state. This similarity helped validate our decision to select principals from one state. Consequently, the test and demographic data available were uniform and complete for each school site in our study.

Table 1.1 describes the selection criteria for the highly successful and comparison principals referred to in this book as well as the fictitious names for the principals and their schools.

LEADERSHIP QUALITIES EXHIBITED

Discussion in the next nine chapters focuses on nine leadership qualities found to be associated with highly successful school principals. Our discussions draw heavily on the information collected during our interviews with principals. At times, we emphasize one highly successful principal who clearly exhibited the featured leadership quality more than the others did. Information gleaned from their interviews dominates the chapters' discussions. On other occasions, information collected from multiple principals highlights the discussion. Information collected during interviews with comparison principals provides contrasting background for the leadership qualities found in highly successful principals.

The discussion of our research on the leadership qualities of highly successful principals begins in Chapter 2 by delving into the one leadership quality not highlighted in Collins' study of successful private sector CEOs: the ability to build relationships. We were surprised to find that this emerged as the prominent leadership quality of every one of the highly successful principals studied.

Table 1.1   Criteria for Selection of Principals to Interview

Criteria for Selection as Highly Successful Principal	Criteria for Selection as Comparison Principal
1. In 1999, his or her school had a California Similar Schools Academic Performance Index (API) decile rank* of 5–8.	1. In 1999, his or her school had a California Similar Schools Academic Performance Index (API) decile rank of 5–8.
2. The principal was assigned to the school during the entire period (from 1999 to 2003).	2. The principal was assigned to the school during the entire period (from 1999 to 2003).
3. In 2001–2003, his or her school had a California Similar Schools API rank of 9 or 10 (two or more deciles higher than in 1999). The principal had made the leap from good to great.	3. Subsequent California Similar Schools API ranks remained the same or fluctuated. The principal had failed to make and maintain the leap from good to great.

Highly Successful Principals	Schools	Comparison Principals	Schools
Ms. Discipline	Eagle Elementary	Ms. Oblivious	Roosevelt Elementary
Mr. Unpretentious	Bay View Elementary	Ms. Conspiracy	Observatory Elementary
Ms. Aspiration	Mission Elementary	Ms. Helpless	Elm Elementary
Mr. Focus	Pines Elementary	Ms. Relinquish	Johnson Elementary
Ms. Persevere	Mountain High Elementary	Ms. Ineffectual	Sunkist Elementary
Mr. Bond	Field Elementary		

* In the California Similar Schools Academic Performance Index (API) ranking system, schools are compared to schools with like demographics such as mobility, credentialed teachers, language, average class size, multitrack year-round schedule, ethnicity, and free or reduced price meals. The highest rank is 10. More information concerning the API is found in Resource B.

REFLECTION

What are some of the most common barriers to school success in your district? Why do some schools succeed in spite of these barriers? What are the critical differences between public schools and private sector businesses? Are the principles of excellent management in the private sector applicable to the management of public schools?

2

First, Build Relationships

No matter what accomplishments you make, somebody helped you.

—Althea Gibson, athlete and author (1927–2003)

I n the private sector, where making a profit is the goal, leaders are not normally required to exert extraordinary effort building relationships because they usually have the luxury of "getting the right people on the bus, the wrong people off the bus, and the right people in the right seats." Unfortunately, public education leaders usually do not have that luxury and must often work with a staff that they did not personally select. Student learning is the goal and people are the mechanisms for producing and sustaining student achievement. For this reason, a key prescription for principal leadership is the ability to work with people and build relationships with teachers, students, parents, and the community. Murphy and Beck (1994) put it this way: "Principals must find their authority in their personal, interpersonal, and professional competencies, not in formal positions; they must cultivate collegiality, cooperation, and shared commitments among all with whom they work" (p. 15).

A BEHAVIOR DIFFERENT FROM THE BEHAVIORS OF THE LEVEL 5 EXECUTIVE

The researchers in Collins' (2001) study of *Good to Great* companies were not looking for leadership as a necessary ingredient when they began their study of successful companies. The finding that the CEOs of each of the *Good to Great* companies shared certain leadership characteristics and that the CEOs of comparison companies did not have these characteristics was a big surprise to Collins' research team. While we were replicating Collins' research protocol with school principals, we were not entirely surprised, given what we know about the importance of relationships in schools, when the ability to build relationships jumped off the page as the most prominent leadership characteristic for every highly successful principal in our study. Building relationships did not surface significantly in the Collins research for either Level 5 Executives or the comparison group CEOs.

When relationships improve, schools get better. If relationships remain the same or get worse, schools regress. "To develop a community of difference, education leaders must take responsibility for developing a meaningful relationship with each person they encounter—student, teacher, parent, board member, or legislator" (Shields, 2004, p. 39). Thus, leaders build relationships with diverse people and groups—especially with people who think differently. Focusing on relationships is not a gimmick for improving student test scores for the next year, but rather a means of laying the foundation for sustaining improvement over the long run. The principal's efforts to motivate and invigorate estranged teachers and to build relationships among otherwise disengaged teachers can have a profound effect on the overall climate of the school. As Michael Fullan (2002) pointed out, "Well-established relationships are the resource that keeps on giving" (p. 18).

School leaders matter because they have the clout to mold conversations—the topic and how that topic is talked about—by resolutely offering their values and goals to others and by articulating in clear emphatic sentences. Leaders also matter because they help to shape a school's culture in ways that promote learning, collaboration, and environments in which all members of the school community feel cared for and respected.

The highly successful principals we interviewed were skilled in just that way when building relationships and promoting leadership, teacher efficacy, and professionalism with their staff. At their schools, collective capacity was the norm.

The educational literature is extensive in support of the benefits of collaboration both for the individual teacher and for school improvement (Darling-Hammond, 1997; DuFour, Eaker, & DuFour, 2005; Little, 1990). Yet, in spite of accepted research, teachers in North America are more likely to be observed working in isolation, teaching discrete groups of students. Whatever the reason for teacher isolation, collaboration will never become the norm in schools unless educators take steps to ensure that collaboration is routine.

One highly successful principal in particular, Mr. Bond, revealed his belief that teacher collaboration should be routine and, if you build relationships, you will create a community of difference.

MR. BOND AND FIELD ELEMENTARY SCHOOL

Who is Mr. Bond, and how did he stir up such a commotion at Field Elementary School? To understand the leadership qualities of Mr. Bond, we look first at his school. Field Elementary School is located near a military base, situated on a hill with open fields on all sides. You can almost see the ocean from the front doors of the school. The well-maintained facilities date from the mid-1960s, and the school currently serves approximately 500 students in Grades K–5. Seven years ago, the district opened a new school and 10 of the teaching staff at Field Elementary transferred to that new school. Then, a year later, the school lost its sixth-grade students due to a district restructuring of all of its elementary and middle schools. Most of the students at Field Elementary are dependents of military personnel. Most parents are young enlisted personnel with high school diplomas.

Because military families are transferred frequently to new locations, the student population is highly mobile, with most of the students moving within two years. Forty-seven percent of the students qualify for free or reduced price meals. A small fraction of parents is not military but works on the base. Approximately 55% of the students are white, 16% are African American, and 20% are Hispanic. The student population of this school is in a constant state of transition; yet its success in increasing student achievement has been consistently high over the past five years. It was not always this way.

The district hired Mr. Bond in 1985 as an assistant principal in the high school. He remained in that position for four years and eventually became principal of one of the district's many elementary schools. About seven years ago, the superintendent decided to reassign many of the principals and thought Mr. Bond would be a good match for Field Elementary School. He has been at this school nestled in the hills overlooking the Pacific Ocean for seven years. The school inherited by Mr. Bond boasted dedicated teachers who worked hard but who did so in isolation from one another. While the student population at Field Elementary School was highly mobile, the teachers at the school tended to stay until they retired from the district.

Mr. Bond toots the horn of his teachers because they are dealing with a high student mobility rate (about 79% of the student population moves in a given year), and they are producing sustained gains in student achievement. Field Elementary has the honor of having earned the Distinguished Schools Award, the Blue Ribbon School Award, and the Title I Achievement Award. Phenomenal progress was demonstrated when their relative Academic Performance Index (API) rank moved from a decile 6 in 1999 to a decile 9 in 2003. In this relative ranking, a school's API is compared to all other schools in the state of California. Even more impressive are the school's similar school API rankings for the years 1999 through 2004, as shown in Table 2.1. The school's rank moved to a 10, the highest rank possible, and stayed there.

Table 2.1   Field Elementary School: API Similar Schools Rank

1999	2000	2001	2002	2003	2004
7	10	10	10	10	10

This success story is not about a particular program as much as it is about the evolution of who the principal and faculty are as a unified group. Mr. Bond attributes the success of his school in improving student achievement performance to this evolution as evidenced by interview responses that follow:

Q: Tell me a little about the teachers of the school and how they have evolved since the first year of the California API.

Mr. B: I think it was 97–98 when the state came down with its first list of underperforming schools. We were on the list. Our API at that time was about 585 [out of 800] and we had just jumped to 637 when the news of our being on the list came out. So it was a little hard to take on the part of the teachers. At the same time, we were fortunate to be funded to make improvement. As a result of being funded we ended up contracting with a consulting program out of UCLA.

We should explain that the Immediate Intervention Underperforming Schools Program was implemented by the State of California to identify and assist schools where student performance was inadequate. Schools participating in that program must meet their program's definition of significant growth, based on the results of the schoolwide API, or the school will be state monitored. In this case, the school may receive state funds to assist in developing a plan of action and implementation of the plan. Field Elementary School was one such school.

When we asked what happened when the consultants arrived, Mr. Bond shrugged as he formulated his answer.

> **Mr. B:**   We had some real critical issues to deal with and did a lot of self-reflection. What was most interesting—and this is the lead-in to your question about the evolution of the staff—was to, as a whole staff, begin to look at what we needed in order to improve what we were doing in the classroom.

The critical issues faced by Field Elementary School staff prompted this principal to consider ways to bring the otherwise isolated teachers together as a cohesive force.

> **Q:**   I thought you said that you had already begun to make changes, and that the jump in API scores was evidence of that?

> **Mr. B:**   I know, that is the ironic part. We were already on the right road as we could see when we jumped from 585 to 637. I said to them, "The nice thing is the message is bittersweet. Being told you are underperforming is tough to take but being labeled that will make us better in the end because now we have the funding to continue what we already started." So, with the help of consultants, we ended up getting into several task forces where every staff member was involved. That was the genesis of our beginning to break down the walls of isolation and building up the foundation of collaboration. And, that's not always easy to do.

Mr. Bond saw that a major barrier to building positive relations with the staff was the lack of communication between school administration and the teachers. When we asked him to clarify what the problems were, he responded slowly and thoughtfully.

> **Mr. B:**   I mean there was a lack of communication between administration and the teaching staff. So, it is one of those moments where we had to grow together. One of the things that I realized and I've come across is that when you look at the qualities of a good leader, you end up with issues like establishing a vision and communicating that vision: rallying the people around that vision, being a great instructional leader. However, I think the Number One quality of a good leader is humbleness.

This last statement led to a continuing conversation between interviewers and principal about the connection between communication and being humble. Mr. Bond was quick to admit his discomfort when, during a planned workshop on building communication skills, he was subject to humiliating criticism in front of his staff. However, he straightaway shared his belief that going through an experience like that helped to bring the staff closer together and enabled them to feel safe in communicating their expectations of one another—something he and his staff very much needed.

Q: What about communication brought you to the importance of being humble?

Mr. B: I soon realized that one of the important things is that, much like a family, you need to do things to grow together and work together. That's exactly what we did that year. We grew together. We were able to put things out there, in terms of what we expect of each other when we talk with each other.

Q: So you had all these things going on—task force meetings, communication workshops. How were you all able to cope with so many changes at once?

Mr. Bond paused reflectively before he answered.

Mr. B: It is never easy but through all of this, we started to act like a family, so when people had issues or concerns we'd say, "Let's talk about this. Let's see what we can do. It is something we need to do together."

We asked Mr. Bond to cite more examples of collaboration and communication. His description of his staff's evolution from being isolated in their classrooms to collaborating as a team indicated that the process was gradual—much like the case of Collins' (2001) "flywheel" concept described earlier. His face reflected pride as he described how his staff evolved.

Mr. B: Oh yes. The staff designed a program where every week grade-level teams have an opportunity to collaborate for 45 minutes during the instructional day each week. We have been doing this for four years. These meetings help to strengthen relationships between grade levels, between teachers and administration, and within teacher teams. We have also come up with what we call Faculty Collaboration Meetings. Another staff member of a grade-level team or I bring up an issue. We discuss it, spend time self-reflecting, come to agreement in grade levels, and then to agreement with the whole staff if needed. At the end of all this, I say "Now read the information items at the end of the agenda."

At the beginning of the interview, Mr. Bond had been asked to talk about how his staff evolved. He returned to that topic.

Mr. B: At the beginning of this interview, you asked me to talk about the evolution of the staff. Well, here it is. Six years ago, we wouldn't have been able to have these grade-level collaborative meetings or Faculty Collaboration Meetings because we didn't know how to talk to one another or collaborate or share with each other.

Q: What have you learned about leadership in all this?

Mr. B: I realize my job is much more than instruction, textbooks, budget, or facilities.

Q: What *is* your job all about then?

Mr. B: My job is all about relationships—my relationships with teachers, teachers with teachers, teachers with students, students with students, and all of us with parents and the community. We can get to curriculum issues through relationships.

Conversation with Mr. Bond continued with a discussion of his leadership style. He revealed that his style is one of collaboration and shared decision making through consensus. He knows this would not be possible at Field Elementary School if it had not been for his evolution and the evolution of his staff. His responses also show that he has patience when decision making as a team does take longer than it would if he made the decision himself.

Mr. B: It is important to do all of those [leadership] duties at the right time, at the right place, and with the right people. Sometimes we need to make decisions together through consensus, but sometimes I have to make the decision. Sometimes [the teachers] make the decision and I support it. For example, the budget was tight and required cutting personnel. It was not wise to simply tell the staff that an instructional aide had to be let go. Instead, we looked at the budget together and they came to that decision themselves. It was a long and tough process because it involved cutting a person they liked. That process took almost four months but we came to the decision as a team. It would have taken no time at all if I had done it myself.

A hallmark of very successful executives is that their ambitions are not for themselves but for the organization. They want to see the company even more successful after they are gone. Mr. Bond revealed this quality when he was questioned about the fate of the school should he leave.

Mr. B: I believe the teachers will continue their relationships in collaborating and working as a team even if the funding for their grade-level meetings should go away. I feel like I'm on this train ride, except I'm the caboose hanging on for dear life because these teachers are moving a hundred miles an hour. If the caboose fell off would anyone notice? I hope not.

This is a story of the evolution of an elementary school staff. They grew together. Mr. Bond and his staff were able to communicate their expectations for each other. During the next few years, the faculty continued to grow professionally. The school no longer wears the label of underperforming and test scores continue to rise.

HIGHLY SUCCESSFUL PRINCIPALS AND BUILDING RELATIONSHIPS

All of the highly successful principals in our study demonstrated their skill in building relationships. Mr. Unpretentious, whom you will meet later in this book, considers himself just one of the leaders of his school. When interviewers asked him what he believed contributes to improved student learning at the school, he responded that he thought that the biggest factor contributing to student achievement success is the involvement of all of his teachers in team leadership training. He felt that their participation in this endeavor gave them the confidence and efficacy to share instructional issues with one another.

Another principal we will meet, Mr. Focus of Pines Elementary School, describes his leadership style as "relational."

Mr. F: I think my style is more relational; I build relationships and trust with the staff and work from there. I think relationships are key. Encouraging teachers to be professionals and giving them the latitude to do what they feel they need to do is important. Micromanaging or dictating methodology is definitely not my style. However, I do come to them with problems and challenges and we solve them together.

Mr. Focus has had the luxury of working with self-motivated and highly disciplined teachers from the beginning, so promoting leadership and treating his teachers with professionalism is almost effortless. "Mostly, I let the staff do the solving with my assistance," he said. Mr. Focus thought he had built a trusting relationship with his staff through being a good listener, offering good ideas, and treating his staff as professionals. It is business as usual at Pines Elementary with the teachers expecting that Mr. Focus will be in their classrooms every day observing, and trusting that they will have two-way professional conversations with him about what he observed.

Some of the highly successful principals in our study faced difficult personnel issues at the beginning of their tenure at the school; even so, they were able to unite the staff and get them moving in a constructive direction.

Ms. Aspiration, principal of Mission Elementary School, inherited a few teachers who were actively involved in the activities of the local teachers' association and supported association guidelines through persuasion, sabotage, and threats. These association people thought they controlled the school, and the school was the way they wanted it to be. In supporting that belief, they would go so far as to threaten the new teachers when they attempted to make changes. Ms. Aspiration's battle began with uniting the staff and getting them moving collaboratively toward increasing student achievement. The interviewer asked her how she dealt with this issue. She smiled as she answered.

Ms. A: I used two devices to unite the staff: Competition with other schools and bringing the staff together to implement a new instructional program called cognitive guided instruction. We had a central goal and all of the staff was involved in the goal. We were actually united in competition with other schools in the district.

By the end of the second year, most of the staff could see where they were heading and wanted to go there. Conversations in the staff lounge turned from whining to sharing instructional strategies because now, as in the case of Mr. Bond and his staff, they were making a difference.

Ms. Persevere of Mountain High Elementary School inherited a staff of tenured teachers who believed that student academic performance at the school was adequate and there was no reason to change what they were doing. She was selected as principal of the school to bring excitement back into the classrooms and to raise student performance expectations. The first year she made subtle changes establishing rapport while developing a two-way relationship of trust and support with the teachers. Then she began to implement instructional changes in the primary grades where teachers were more receptive to change. Teachers received support from Ms. Persevere through coaching, modeling lessons, and providing them time to meet to talk about instruction. The principal went to district-sponsored staff development, then turned around and trained the staff in what she learned. As the upper-grade teachers watched the primary-grade teachers collaborate to make changes, some of them became worried and even refused to participate. Ms. Persevere identified people on the staff who were the most resistant. We asked her how she was able to build a positive relationship with those people.

Ms. P: I was careful to figure them out and brought them in ahead of time to talk with them and get their buy-in before meeting with the other teachers. They needed to see the value in something before making a decision.

Ultimately, Ms. Persevere worked with those who were amenable, convincing them that taking risks was not a bad thing. Others, she counseled to transfer to another school or retire.

Ms. Discipline came to a school where the teaching staff was fragmented. The former principal of Eagle Elementary School had played grade levels against grade levels in providing materials and training opportunities. Ms. Discipline was able to shape relationships by providing teachers with joint planning time and by building their self-efficacy in respecting their professional judgments about implementing curriculum. When asked what her leadership style is, she responded with enthusiasm.

Ms. D: I work by encouragement and try to make people feel that taking a risk is not a bad thing. I tell teachers to do what works for them and use materials as a back up, but please don't throw out the baby with the bath water. The objective is to build upon successful experience.

COMPARISON PRINCIPALS AND BUILDING RELATIONSHIPS

When highly successful principals described their experiences in building relationships, they spoke about being part of the family, about being just one of the leaders of the school, and about truly sharing and collaborating with the teachers. In short, they talked about building sound, enduring human relationships. In contrast, the comparison principals seemed to be more isolated in their jobs at the school and less a member of a school family. For example, Ms. Helpless of Elm Elementary School related that the only teacher she really had conversations with on a daily basis was the literacy coach.

Ms. H: It is very hard here to build relationships. You do have relationships but not as close as in other schools I have been in. I don't have conversations with most teachers at this school on a regular basis, not unless I have formally scheduled a meeting.

Another comparison principal, Ms. Ineffectual, said that even though she feels that she is the kind of person that always cares for people, it is difficult to build rapport because of a constant separation between administrators and teachers and students.

Ms. I: There is a separation between administrators and teachers and students that I don't understand. We don't talk to each other on an informal basis. Then there are the students. A youngster said to me, "I don't go to the principal's office. Only bad kids go to the principal's office."

Comparison principals who shared their stories of difficulties with staff seemed resigned to their problems, believing there was no end to their troubles in trying to shape effective relationships at their schools. Ms. Relinquish shared that there were rumors at the school that teachers were afraid to talk to her.

Ms. R: The union people tell me that my teachers don't come to me because they are in fear of retaliation from me. How can that be?

Like their more successful counterparts, comparison principals communicated their beliefs in the value of building relationships, promoting professionalism, and developing leaders. The difference? Highly successful principals could do it!

REFLECTION

Hank Rubin (2002) said, "In public we get things done *with* and *through* people" (p. 14). With regard to school principals you know, what actions have they taken to build the relationships needed to get things done? What criteria would you use to decide which actions are the most important to take in building relationships?

SUGGESTIONS FOR PRINCIPALS

Building Relationships

- Discover the strengths of each member of the staff.
- Develop a meaningful relationship with each person encountered.
- Attempt to develop meaningful relationships with estranged or disengaged staff.
- Openly communicate with staff.

Promoting Teacher Leadership

- Involve staff in decision making. Promote collective capacity, eliminate teacher isolation.
- Promote leadership and professionalism.
- Organize and support professional learning communities.

3

Exercise Your Professional Will, But Stay Humble

There is nothing brilliant or outstanding in my record, except perhaps this one thing. I do the things I believe ought to be done . . . and when I make up my mind to do a thing, I act.

—Theodore Roosevelt, 26th president
of the United States (1858–1919)

T he Level 5 Executives of Collins' (2001) research never let their egos get in the way of their primary ambition for the larger cause of an enduring organization. In keeping with the essence of Roosevelt's quote, "they are a study in duality: modest and willful, humble and fearless" (p. 22). Collins (2004) later commented that the Level 5 Executives of his research were not inspiring personalities and yet their companies were incredibly inspired environments. What they had instead of inspiring personalities were inspired standards. When a person has impeccable standards, these standards inspire. When people see the momentum building from the results of their efforts, they are motivated. Charismatic people can motivate and inspire, but the inspiration is often unsustainable. The real impetus is not in the leader, but in the system and the people in the system. Abraham Lincoln was a study in duality. Those who did not know him perceived his shy, modest nature and awkward manner as signs of weakness. Historical accounts of Lincoln's actions find these perceptions terribly mistaken. He never let his ego get in the way of his primary ambition for the larger cause of an enduring nation (McPherson, 1989).

ISSUES WITH IDENTIFYING PERSONAL HUMILITY IN SCHOOL PRINCIPALS

The duality of professional will and personal humility that Collins (2001) described was not easy to detect in the interview responses of the principals as long as we remained true to Collins' definition of personal humility. Professional will was reflected clearly and often in principal responses to our interview questions. Personal humility was another matter altogether, and warrants discussion before we describe our findings among the principals in our study. We found evidence for personal humility in every one of our highly successful principals. However, that was not clear the first time we examined our interview transcripts. During this first pass-through, we discovered that three of the six highly successful principals (all men) demonstrated personal humility using the criteria we established (self-effacing mannerisms and obvious comments exuding humility, much like the *Good to Great* CEOs); three (all women) did not. This split in the findings was a surprise and caused us to reflect on any biases or misunderstandings of the concept of personal humility that might have been in play during our examinations of the information collected. We stepped back and considered three issues we realized were skewing our efforts: (1) the nature of the interview questions when considering the work of school principals, (2) the shortcomings of interview evidence, and (3) personality differences among principals that could be attributed to gender.

Nature of the Interview Questions

The questions we were asking principals in our study were modified versions of the questions used in Collins' (2001) research. Consequently, we were looking to see whether principal responses followed a similar pattern to the *Good to Great* CEOs in that they would be self-effacing, quiet, reserved, and even shy in their interviews. These CEOs were at the top of a complex hierarchy of leadership in companies that produced profit in dollars as an indicator of their success. Our principals were the leaders of schools where the measure of success was in human factors such as collaborative decision making, effective instructional practices, and increased student performance. Our principals were responding to questions that asked about what they did at the school and what they instituted that might have led to their school's success. In all of the stories heard from these principals, decisions and actions taken were the handiwork of principals working directly with their staffs. It was difficult for them to avoid entirely discussion about their personal part in the success of the school. What separated the highly successful principals from the *Good to Great* CEOs was a more subtle way in which they responded to questions about their actions in working directly with others. Mr. Bond, the highly successful principal whom we got to know in the last chapter, shared that he also grew as the staff evolved. He described a process he and the staff were now using for staff meetings, saying, "As an instructional leader, I have grown tremendously. With this talent [the teachers] I have out there, I could just kick myself for not using that [the staff meeting process] five years ago." He demonstrates his humility in multiple ways in this one series of statements—through the recognition that he had grown along with the staff, his self-effacing acknowledgement that he was to blame for not instituting the staff meeting process years ago, and his appreciation of the talent of the teachers.

Shortcomings of Interview Data

Over several years, the research team in the Collins (2001) study analyzed a variety of evidence in addition to the interview data in coming to the conclusions they did about the CEOs of *Good to Great* companies. Company documents, speeches, newspaper and magazine articles, and interviews of coworkers and others were analyzed. Our examination of highly successful principals came from one source—the interviews we conducted. If the principals we were interviewing did not exhibit outward mannerisms of personal humility, we had one other way of determining this behavior—their spoken words. Fortunately, this produced the information we were seeking.

Personality Differences

Not all of our highly successful principals displayed shy or understated natures during their interviews. Right away that gave us cause to wonder whether the personal humility identified in the Collins (2001) study might not be a factor for our school principals. However, we found in every one of our highly successful principals subtle signs of personal humility, whether they were shy and reserved or unreserved and outgoing. During the individual interviews, differences in the exuberance of the principals were apparent. Table 3.1 describes the range of personality exuberance observed by the interviewer, from placid and reserved to energetic and unreserved.

Table 3.1   Range of Personality Exuberance of the Highly Successful and Comparison Principals

Placid, Calm	← —————————————————→			Energetic, Unreserved
Mr. Focus	Ms. Conspiracy	Ms. Helpless	Ms. Oblivious	Ms. Discipline
Mr. Unpretentious	Ms. Relinquish			Ms. Aspiration
Mr. Bond				Ms. Persevere
Ms. Ineffectual				

An interesting pattern emerged when we analyzed the data represented in Table 3.1. Personality exuberance ranged from a placid, calm demeanor (all three of the highly successful male principals and one female comparison principal) to energetic, unreserved, and enthusiastic (the three highly successful female principals), with the other female comparison principals falling somewhere in between.

Is there a rationale for this division of personality types along gender lines among the highly successful principals? We suspect so. The emergence of women teachers in the 1800s is remarkable. Historically, women were expected to respect and rely on men's authority, so they had little need to be educated (Blount, 1998). In less than 50 years, women had progressed from having few means of employment outside the home to accounting for around 70 percent of all teachers by 1900. Except in the early days of the elementary school principalship, the principalship of schools has been dominated by men. In the early decades of the twentieth century, thousands of women succeeded in attaining school leadership positions (Blount, 1999). Women now comprise about 57% of central office administrators and 41% of principals (Keller, 1999). When considering leadership capability at the elementary school level, modesty or humility in male principals was, and is, considered a sign of strength, especially given the fact that principals work with a predominantly female teaching staff. During our own careers as teachers and school administrators, we have known many women who moved up the ladder of success in a traditionally male-dominated leadership role. In many, if not most, of these cases the women stood out from coworkers by being less reserved, more enthusiastic, and even somewhat aggressive. We suspect that this behavior was a way of combating institutional bias toward male candidates. In other words, the bravado was an attempt to dispel any ideas about female frailty.

PERSONAL HUMILITY: THE EVIDENCE DIFFERS

What did this all mean in terms of identifying personal humility in our principals? At first, we did not know what to think about finding that half of our highly successful principals had placid, calm personalities, as did all of the *Good to Great* CEOs. The other half of our highly successful principals exhibited unreserved, energetic, and even somewhat aggressive personalities. We examined each of the principal transcripts multiple times, looking for signs of humility that were not necessarily obvious, finding many examples with all of our highly successful principals. Then we remembered about the methods Collins (2001) and his research team used to hash out meaning in the information collected. Collins said they met often to "debate, disagree, pound the tables, raise our voices, pause and reflect, debate some more, pause and think, discuss, resolve, question, and debate yet again about 'what it all means'" (p. 10). We came together to discuss the information we collected as a team, first agreeing that Collins' description of personal humility was present in the *Good to Great* CEOs as a constant state of giving the appearance to others of being self-effacing and quiet. Their outward mannerisms clearly exhibited personal humility. We could affirm without hesitation that throughout their interviews, the mannerisms of our three highly successful male principals corresponded to the criteria for personal humility in the Collins study. This was not the case for our three highly successful female principals. For them, personal humility presented itself intermittently in their spoken words, but not in their mannerisms. (We give examples of this later on in this chapter.) We then agreed that, just because the personalities of these three are outgoing and energetic, it is not fair to assume they cannot demonstrate personal humility in other ways. For example, when asked what she was most proud of, Ms. Discipline, who on the surface exhibits an enthusiastic and unreserved manner, quietly stated, "The staff. They care for each other. The willingness to give of themselves professionally and personally. I'm in awe of them." Given this modification in our thinking about personal humility, we can now state that all of our highly successful principals demonstrated personal humility through their personalities or their spoken words, or both.

In our study, where we found evidence for duality of professional will and personal humility, we also found support for other characteristics and behaviors we were studying. Some of the examples we give of the professional will and personal humility of our highly successful principals are referenced again in other chapters as examples of such attributes as compelling modesty, the hedgehog concept, unwavering resolve, and ambition for the organization, to name a few.

We turn now to evidence supporting the presence of a duality of professional will and personal humility in our highly successful principals by looking first at those principals whose personalities were shy and self-effacing.

SHY AND SELF-EFFACING LEADERS

As stated earlier, all three of our male highly successful principals serve as our examples of school leaders who match Collins' description of personal humility. We also defined personal humility as characterized by the self-effacing, quiet, and humble manner of the *Good to Great* CEOs. We scrutinize these three male principals for evidence of a duality of professional will and personal humility.

Mr. Focus

Perhaps Mr. Focus demonstrates most vividly this duality. This principal did not exhibit an inspiring personality. In fact, during the interview he was actually quite shy, unassuming, and serious. The interviewer needed to place the tape recorder microphone very close to him because he spoke quietly. Make no mistake. His shy and unassuming nature was not a sign of a weakness. He wanted what he wanted, and was sure he got it. His response to questions about hiring teachers when his school first opened was an illustration of his professional will. He shared his philosophy with each prospective teacher and, if they did not share his philosophy, they were not selected for the new school. When asked about reasons for the success of his school, Mr. Focus was adamant about the efforts he made but responded with humility while he reaffirmed his professional will.

Mr. F: I would hope people would know that I did everything possible to support teachers in making sure students were successful at our school. That was my Number One priority.

He shared a passion regarding standards for teaching students to read. Mr. Focus was determined that all financial and instructional decisions made at Twin Pines Elementary School were about providing what was necessary in order for students to read well. His teachers clearly understood his standards and were inspired. Then, when his teachers saw the momentum building from the results of their efforts in teaching reading and in providing opportunities for students to read, they continued to be motivated. Mr. Focus' resolve that teachers were successful in effectively teaching their students was enhanced by his function in the decision-making processes at the school. Decision making was collegial but no nonsense and clearly demonstrated the professional will of Mr. Focus.

Mr. F: Decision making was a group effort. [The assistant principal and I] were honest with teachers about decisions that needed to be made. My job was to lead the process. I'd go in with an end in mind . . . one that I had really thought through. Whatever the teachers decided to do, most of the time it was close to what I would have chosen to do. If their decision was off, which almost never happened, we'd talk about it and keep on talking about it until their decision fit our agreed upon way of thinking.

Even though Mr. Focus was strong willed when it came to his own convictions, he would be the first to tell anyone that the system at Pines Elementary and the people in that system are what caused that momentum, not the principal alone.

Mr. Bond

Like Mr. Focus, Mr. Bond displayed an understated, self-effacing manner. He presented himself as humble in the way he carried himself during our interview. This was a man who gave the appearance of having a calm, laid-back, low-key disposition simply by the way he sat in his chair. Our chairs were set up facing each other, without a desk in between. His back was to a wall so he could see out the open door to the rest of the office while focusing his attention on the interviewer. He sat in a relaxed position with arms folded. Throughout the interview, he was very quiet and only spoke when asked a question. Once a question was asked, Mr. Bond took his time to answer, seemingly weighing various aspects before he responded. His responses were slow and measured and, much like Mr. Focus, he spoke so softly that the tape recorder microphone had to be clipped to his tie in order to pick up his words. Whereas outwardly he exhibited personal humility, his responses clearly witnessed his professional will. He chuckled as he recalled a rather negative experience he had had with his supervisor.

Mr. B: Four years ago, it was time for my annual evaluation. My school's test scores were flat. My boss called me into his office and said, "Either get it together or you're fired." That was tough to take. When I walked out of this initial evaluation session, I called my mentor. He asked, "Did you ever think you were off course in your vision of what you were trying to do with the school?"

"No."

"You were true to yourself?"

"Yes."

"Then, that is the best you can do. Sometimes [the evaluation] is not so much a reflection of what you are to the district as much as it is that you may no longer be a match [for the district]. Never see yourself as a victim."

And I didn't. I did not change. The irony is, all of a sudden our API [Academic Performance Index] scores went up and we were one of the first "800" (API score) schools in the district. . . . The boss called me in a year and a half later and I got a glowing evaluation, as though the first negative evaluation never happened. As humbly as I could, I reached out my hand to him and said, "Thank you so much." It's all about life's peaks and valleys.

Strong evidence for the duality of his professional will and personal humility presented itself when Mr. Bond was asked about his leadership style. He responded hesitantly.

Mr. B: That depends on whom you ask. I hope they would tell you that I am fair more than anything else. They would probably say that I am calm and a good listener. They would say, "He likes to laugh at himself and share personal stories about himself." I guess they would describe me as someone who sits back, listens, and then reacts to what I hear in a calm manner. They would also say that I don't change course once I say I'm going to do something.

Mr. Unpretentious

The events that transpired when we entered the front office of Bay View Elementary School we describe in the next chapter when we introduce you to Mr. Unpretentious' school and go into more depth with the *Good to Great* characteristic of compelling modesty. However, just now you need to understand what sort of manner of man Mr. Unpretentious is. Mr. Unpretentious had an understated and reserved nature as evidenced during our interview session with him. Throughout the interview, Mr. Unpretentious spoke slowly and meticulously, something the interviewer very much appreciated, given the need to type his responses into a laptop while recording every word.

We have just introduced you briefly to his humble nature. We look now at the other half of the duality: professional will. Evidence for the professional will of Mr. Unpretentious surfaced when he spoke about his ambitions for the teachers of his school. Mr. Unpretentious understood his primary clients were the teachers of his school and that his job was to support them, protect them, and encourage them. Through them, students achieved. He believed that when you create teacher self-efficacy and confidence, you ensure that classroom instruction will be the best it can be and that students will learn. Hence, Mr. Unpretentious took on the task of building leadership among his teachers. He made this task a priority for the school and continued with that priority.

Mr. U: I put a lot of effort into being sure this school is run by shared leadership. I see my main responsibility here is to support the people who do the real work in classrooms. I also work to make certain these same people are sharing with me the responsibility for making the important decisions here. To do that, we all needed a lot of training. I went with my teachers to every one of those trainings.

Mr. Unpretentious exhibited professional will in supporting his teachers.

Mr. U: I am also not afraid to go to bat for my teachers when issues from outside the school are making their work tougher. I got a call from the superintendent's office recently telling me that a parent had called his office directly to complain about one of my teachers. I got in my car and drove to the central office, did some research on the issue, and found out that the complaint was unjustified. The teacher never found out that there was a complaint.

UNRESERVED AND ENTHUSIASTIC LEADERS

As divulged earlier, the three highly successful female principals in our study provided a very different picture from the calm and reserved male principals. All three of these principals exuded energetic, enthusiastic, and unreserved personalities. Since their personalities clearly are not shy and reserved, we decided to look more closely at their responses to our interview questions. We examined Ms. Persevere's interview first.

Ms. Persevere

We examined Ms. Persevere's interview and found that, for her and for all of our highly successful principals, resolve and professional go hand in hand. Ms. Persevere demonstrated professional will often in her responses. Her responses to questions about the teaching staff of her school and how they evolved were straightforward and commanding.

Ms. P: I made very subtle changes establishing rapport, gaining trust, and being supportive while learning about everyone's programs. Then I could immediately match my concerns with test data and that gave me ammunition for the following year.

When asked about her leadership style, Ms. Persevere spoke about ways she would get buy-in from the staff.

Ms. P: I believe that the more I talk with teachers, the more buy-in I get. For instance, there are some teachers on the staff habitually sabotaging efforts by other teachers. I know who these teachers are and have private conversations with them often in order to get their buy-in ahead of time. This tactic pays off. Conversations at staff meetings go nowhere if I go to the meeting cold without bringing these people in first. Negative comments by a few carry little influence around here.

Ms. Persevere believed that she could not expect teachers to do things if she was not willing to do them herself. Because she was certain that whatever they had all agreed to implement was for the good of student learning, she did everything to support the teachers' efforts. She would model lessons and coach teachers, provide resources, and organize staff development to support them.

This principal shared factors that she believed were humbling for her.

Ms. P: The first year [of my tenure at the school] we created a vision and mission statement. I had already spent a year working on my own vision. My vision was my vision. I had my rose-colored glasses on. I quickly realized we needed to spend time developing a collective school vision.

Ms. Aspiration

Ms. Aspiration's professional will is rooted in her ambition for the success of the school. Her leadership at Mission Elementary School was marked by the presence of a divided faculty consisting of stubborn tenured teachers and eager new teachers.

Ms. A: These old people fought me from the start. One actually said, "We make or break principals here at Mission Elementary." I did not let it get to me. I figured that when it was all over and done with, the school would be successful, whether they liked me or not.

When asked about her leadership style she sat up in her chair and in a direct and confident manner said, "I'm very open with the staff about my feelings and sometimes that can get you in trouble. . . . I believe in what I believe in, and I am going to fight for it."

Ms. Aspiration shared one prior experience related to work that she believes helped shape her leadership. Her personal humility, which had thus far in the interview been somewhat masked by her professional will, energy, and competitive spirit, came out here.

Ms. A: Some of the trials and tribulations of the first school where I was principal helped me. When I got my first principal job in this district, I knew everything I was doing I was doing right. When I would not back down, that was tough. I learned that you couldn't make people do things unless they are ready. You learn from your hard knocks. I sure did.

Ms. Discipline

Last, we turn to Ms. Discipline whose enthusiasm radiated with every comment she made. We felt this same energy permeating the atmosphere of her school the moment we walked through the front doors and found ourselves caught up in her zeal often during our conversation with her.

Ms. Discipline described her own reaction—evidence of her professional will—to occasions early on in her tenure at Eagle Elementary School where certain members of her teaching staff demonstrated negative attitudes and behaviors. There were teachers on the first-grade team who had been very close to the previous principal, who were not making life very pleasant for anybody. She made a conscious decision that she would not allow them to change the path she was taking in building a culture of discipline at her school.

When asked about the district hiring process and what freedom she had, if any, to make staffing selections, Mr. Discipline shared what she called "the bane of her existence."

Ms. D: In the spring, all 14 of the principals meet for panel interviews of prospective teachers. It's really about who needs what. Sometimes going in I say, "I'm picking these people. They are mine. Forget it. End of discussion."

Ms. Discipline adds that people who know her are well aware of her just plain stubbornness in obtaining the very best for her school.

On the other hand, evidence for personal humility was not difficult to discern in the responses of Ms. Discipline to our questions. Tears welled up as she spoke of the way the school works.

Q: When you are thinking of your work here, what are you most proud of?

Ms. D: The staff—their caring for each other and willingness to give of themselves professionally and personally.

COMPARISON PRINCIPALS

The comparison principals did not exhibit the same fearlessness or willfulness of the highly successful principals. In at least two cases, the principals would actually step aside on some issues that were important to them to avoid confrontation. Ms. Helpless voiced her frustrations with the few members of her staff who use the union contract to stop any positive moves toward change. She remarked, "I know what should happen and what our next steps should be, but I've got this negative group of teachers. It's like we are moving and they are pulling the strings of the train back. Maybe I should just transfer to another school." Ms. Relinquish responded to a question asking her how she deals with pressures of accountability by saying, "You just shake your head and move on."

Modesty or humility is not to be confused with the frustration and feelings of resignation or defeat expressed by most of the comparison principals at some point in their interviews. Ms. Ineffectual was the exception, as she remarked, "I'm a person who works right along with the staff. I feel I am a learner too. I don't feel like I have all the answers."

REFLECTION

Think about an educational leader you know who exhibits the qualities of both professional will and personal humility. Are there actions of professional will or personal humility, or both, that this person displays that others could learn? What activities could serve as a learning exercise for these qualities?

SUGGESTIONS FOR PRINCIPALS

Exhibiting Professional Will

- Be fearless.
- Act as a buffer between school and external forces.
- Be adamant.
- Voice priorities.

Exhibiting Personal Humility

- Be humble.
- Be self-effacing.
- Be quick to praise others.
- Be unassuming.

4

Credit Others, Accept the Blame

The greatest ornament of an illustrious life is modesty and humility, which go a great way in the character even of the most exalted princes.

—Napoleon I, French emperor (1769–1821)

Collins' (2001) Level 5 Executives talked about their companies and the contributions of others, but avoided discussion about the part they personally played. When things go well, they give credit to others; when things go badly, they accept the blame. Conversely, Collins studied comparison companies where the *I*-centric or charismatic self-interested style of the top leader led them to blame others for failures and credit themselves for success.

Some studies show that an *I*-centric or charismatic style is not necessarily a positive trait for educational leaders. Murphy (1988) in his studies of educational leadership and its effect on schools said, "Where heroism is concerned, less can be more. To be a lamb is really to be a lion" (p. 659). Fullan and Hargreaves (1991) offered this perspective on *I*-centricity versus humility:

> "My vision," "my teachers," "my school" are proprietary claims and attitudes that suggest an ownership of the school that is personal rather than collective, imposed rather than earned, and hierarchical rather than democratic. It reduces the opportunities for principals to learn that parts of their own vision may be flawed, and that some teachers' visions may be as valid or more valid than theirs may. (p. 90)

We suggest here that an *I*-centric school principal will be instrumental in setting the stage at a school in such a way that collective capacity cannot be sustained and leadership among teachers will not be promoted.

ADDITIONAL DATA FOR COMPELLING MODESTY

On an impulse, or perhaps because we read about this technique elsewhere, we conducted an experiment of sorts to further determine the presence or absence of an *I*-centric style in the principals we studied. We tallied the number of times each of the principals began his or her statements with the word "I" in response to the questions that focused on the factors contributing to their school's success and decisions the school made to initiate an increase in student achievement. As a group, the highly successful principal "I" tally was 31 while the comparison principal total was 58. Although the sample size is small and the variables are many, the difference in "I" tallies is a smidgen more kindling to support our belief that the highly successful principals as a group were more modest about their role in the success of their school than were the comparison principals.

EVIDENCE FOR SUSTAINABILITY OF GREATNESS

Important to Collins' (2001) findings about the CEOs in his study was the sustainability of the greatness of the company after the CEO leaves. Studies have examined the effect that charismatic leadership has on continuation of program goals after the leader leaves the organization. Lewin and Regine (as cited in Fullan, 2001) asserted, "The ultimate leadership contribution is to develop leaders in the organization who can move the organization even further after you have left" (p. 220). Fullan (1992) hypothesized that most schools decline after the "powerhouse" leader leaves (p. 19). In later writings (2001), he made the following observation:

> Charismatic leaders inadvertently often do more harm than good because, at best, they provide episodic improvement followed by frustrated or despondent dependency. Superhuman leaders also do us another disservice: they are role models who can never be emulated by large numbers. Deep and sustained reform depends on many of us, not just on the very few who are destined to be extraordinary. (p. 2)

What has happened to the successful schools in our study since we last visited them? All of these schools continue to produce impressive student achievement results even when their highly successful principals have moved on to other schools or to district level positions.

EVIDENCE FOR COMPELLING MODESTY

You will remember that the questions we asked principals in our study were modified versions of the questions used in Collins' research. Given that, we expected principal responses to follow a similar pattern to the *Good to Great* CEOs in that they would avoid discussions about the part they played in a given effort. Our principals responded to questions about what they did at the school and what they instituted that might have led to their school's success. It was difficult for them to avoid entirely discussion about the part they played in the success of the school. What separated the highly successful principals from the comparison principals was a subtle modesty in the way they responded to questions. They consistently gave credit to the work of teachers at their schools and took blame personally for decisions or programs that failed. Examples from Ms. Aspiration and Ms. Persevere follow:

Ms. A: [When timed math tests got in the way of doing other, more relevant, math activities] the teachers figured out that they could continue doing the timed tests but just not so often and that the test times should be adjusted for individual student needs. I had nothing to do with that decision.

Ms. P: [When some of the teachers at Mountain High Elementary School grumbled about having to implement guided reading every day] I was pushing them too fast. So, I backed off.

Comparison principals sometimes gave credit to teachers but often demonstrated frustration by blaming other factors or people when things did not work out the way they intended. For instance, when her staff was told that a math program they wanted to continue using was being eliminated, Ms. Conspiracy had this as an excuse:

Ms. C: It wasn't my fault. When the superintendent said it had to go, it went.

We relate evidence for compelling modesty among our highly successful principals, beginning with Mr. Unpretentious and Bay View Elementary School.

MR. UNPRETENTIOUS AND BAY VIEW ELEMENTARY SCHOOL

Bay View Elementary School is one of 12 schools in one California school district. The school services approximately 700 students in Grades K–6. Bay View Elementary is located on 10 acres of land, two miles from the Pacific Ocean. A beautiful little city park borders the school on one side. The facilities of this school date from the mid-1950s with many temporary classrooms on the grounds. Approximately 65% of the students are Hispanic, 14% are white, 14% are Filipino, and the rest (7%) are African American and other. Thirty-one percent of the students are English language learners whose home languages are either Spanish or Filipino (95% and 5% of the English language learners, respectively). Forty-three percent of the students qualify for free or reduced price meals. The district has designated the school as an overflow school. Students displaced because their school of residence is at capacity are transported to Bay View Elementary. Even with this unique status and the resulting highly mobile student population, the school's Academic Performance Index (API) similar schools ranking has continued to be extraordinary, as shown in Table 4.1.

Table 4.1   Bay View Elementary School: API Similar Schools Rank

1999	2000	2001	2002	2003	2004	2005
7	10	10	10	9	9	9

Our arrival at the Bay View Elementary School front office on interview day began by leaving us somewhat befuddled. Men and women were moving busily around the office, conversing about typical end-of-the-day issues— two students missed the bus, the person who was supposed to teach the afterschool art program didn't show, the third-grade teachers were meeting in room #2 to go over test results. Initially, no one stepped forward to greet us. We certainly could not tell who the principal was. Finally, a gentleman behind the reception counter asked in an unassuming manner, "Can I help you?" By then we had figured out which of the side offices belonged to the principal and, with glances to the side, were looking for evidence of someone in that office. We replied by identifying who we were and that we had an appoint-ment with the principal. The gentleman who greeted us answered, "I'm Don Unpretentious. I guess I'm the one you're here to see."

In no time, we were immersed in conversation with Mr. Unpretentious. We soon learned that he has been employed continuously with the district for 27 years. About 10 years before our interview, he had been promoted to principal of an elementary school in the district, where he remained for five years. When asked why he believed he was selected to serve as prin-cipal in the district, Mr. Unpretentious implied that it was not anything he really did that got him the job. His modest comments went like this:

Mr. U: I think I got the principalship in the district initially because the super-intendent wanted principals to have their doctorate. I was working on it at the time and I guess that impressed the superintendent.

Q: Why do you think you were assigned the Bay View Elementary School principalship?

Mr. U: The district has a process where principals are moved every five years. It was my turn to move. It wasn't anything that I did.

We wanted to understand what transpired at Bay View Elementary School during its transition to greatness.

Q: Talk a little about the staff of the school and how they have evolved in the past five years.

Mr. U: When I came to Bay View Elementary School, I inherited a staff of 42 teachers. At least half of them were relative beginners [one to three years' of experience). At that time, the school was on multitrack year-round. It was virtually impossible to get the staff together because at least one-third of the staff was always off track. Teachers had become isolated from each other. It was almost as though the school had three disjointed staffs. A year later, the school went to single-track year-round. I saw this as an opportunity to do some things to bring the staff together, to collaborate, to share decision making.

This was a chance to get at the heart of what this principal and his staff did differently after going single-track year-round that affected an increase in student achievement. Mr. Unpretentious was asked about factors that influenced student achievement at Bay View Elementary School. His responses confirmed that he operated from the premise that leadership should be widely dispersed throughout a school, thus developing the lead-ership potential of all staff members. He was skilled at building the faculty relationships needed for effective collaboration between teachers and him. He understood the value in spawning teacher efficacy through building collective leadership capacity.

Q: In 2000, your school's API similar schools ranking jumped from a 7 to a 10. Why do you think that happened?

Mr. Unpretentious appeared puzzled with this question at first, but then responded with conviction.

Mr. U: Well, it was because of the good teaching staff. They really made an effort. That year we were the highest in the county in our growth.

Q: Did you change your academic program or make any other change in the way you and your staff did things that might have affected student achievement?

Mr. U: What we did do that year and for the next four years in a row was get involved with the County Office of Education and its school leadership teams. Representative members from every grade level and I met all year long at these county meetings. I think we met every month and then would come back to the school to meet with grade-level teams to disseminate all the information we got.

The teaching staff's involvement with school leadership teams at the County Office of Education resulted in a cohesive school leadership team of which Mr. Unpretentious was simply one member.

Mr. U: It was the first time that teachers really were sitting down and sharing ideas about the work they do with students. I think this could happen because the teachers had a greater feeling of self-efficacy going through the leadership team program. We are all working collectively now; to me that has the biggest impact on student achievement of all. They've continued to work together in this way ever since.

Q: What do you do to ensure that teachers continue to focus on improving student test performance? How do you know they follow through in the classroom?

Mr. U: By me getting into classrooms to see how teachers are implementing what they say they want to do. Then I tell them what I learned by being in their classrooms. I am not going into classrooms to spy— just collect the data teachers need to better inform their teaching.

When asked about his leadership style, he was true to his character in crediting the dedication and hard work of the staff. Consider the following interview discourse:

Mr. U: I don't think of myself as the leader of the school. I think of myself as just one of the leaders at this school. It's really them, not me. If they were not doing the work, the work would not be done. They are the ones in the trenches.

Q: What do you do as "just one of the leaders of the school"?

Mr. U: Well, what I do is involve people. This school runs by shared leadership. I give teachers release time so they can work together. Everybody is involved in something. Whenever there is an important decision to be made, I pull in all the people involved.

Mr. Unpretentious credited the teacher leaders with making most decisions.

Mr. U: I can't remember a time when I made a decision on my own. Well, I guess there might be times when a decision is so minor that I don't want to waste people's time.

As this principal talked about the importance he placed on protecting teachers from external mandates, he downplayed his role.

Q: How does your school manage the pressures of district, state, and federal accountability while making long-term changes for the future?

Mr. U: I know that I do not put additional pressure on them. I don't bring [external test scores] up unless I have to.

Q: What do you do instead?

Mr. U: We talk more about improving student achievement in the larger context because that is what we do this for—not necessarily AYP [adequate yearly progress, which is a statewide accountability system mandated by the No Child Left Behind Act of 2001] or API, or some other program labels; the teachers are the ones doing it all. I just need to do what I can to protect them from all those other pressures.

Besides crediting others for successes, evidence for compelling modesty is in taking the blame for things that do not work. Mr. Unpretentious is first to take the blame for a situation recently when the local media focused on only the poor test results of the English language learners at his school. He stared out the window as he contemplated his answer.

Mr. U: I feel bad about the English language learners having to be tested in English. I should have been better at publicizing SABE/2 [Spanish Assessment of Basic Education, which is the California-mandated test for Spanish speakers] results where they could show they are, in fact, learning to read and solve math problems.

The conversation with this highly successful principal ended the way it had proceeded the entire interview session, with Mr. Unpretentious giving credit to the teachers for the school's success and in thinking about what will happen in the future.

Q: What are you most proud of when thinking about your work at Bay View Elementary?

Mr. U: Everybody works together so well and supports each other. It's a good place to come to work to . . . and that's because of the staff, not because of anything I've done.

Q: What do you think will happen to the school's work if you were to leave?

Mr. U: I don't think the school will change much if I leave. The leadership team is so strong. Besides, it is really the teachers, not me.

HIGHLY SUCCESSFUL PRINCIPALS AND COMPELLING MODESTY

All of the highly successful principals gave credit to others and accepted the blame when things were not going well. We look again to Mr. Bond, who is inclined to credit the work of his teachers or a given situation that may have occurred. When we visited his school, a bulletin board display in the school office caught our attention. The display contained the California Distinguished Schools Award plaque surrounded by photos of each of the staff members of the school. There was no photo of Mr. Bond among the photos.

Q: May I ask why your photo is not included on the California Distinguished Schools Award plaque in the front office?

Mr. B: Why should my photo be up there? I didn't do anything.

When it was clear that he and his staff needed to come out from the isolation of their classrooms to build relationships and communicate more, he participated in workshops along with his teachers. He was quick to describe the experience as a personally humbling event when he and his staff grew together and when he developed as an instructional leader. He blames himself for not building relationships and orchestrating conversations with his staff earlier.

Mr. B: I could just kick myself for not using [staff agendas] the way I should have been using [them] five years earlier . . . and [collaborative conversation] was always there . . . and again another humbling experience for me was to realize it will always be there. It is up to me to orchestrate conversations coming out.

COMPARISON PRINCIPALS AND COMPELLING MODESTY

Comparison principals also credited successes to the teachers or other staff members. However, during our interviews, they sometimes placed blame for failures on others, such as the teachers' union, parents, tenured teachers, district superintendent, or language difficulties of the students. Here is a sample of responses from comparison principals Ms. Oblivious, Ms. Relinquish, and Ms. Helpless to the question, "What have you tried at your school that hasn't worked?"

Ms. O: Sometimes things that I feel are important sort of peter out because teachers want to do something different.

Ms. R: [I had asked the teachers to consider opening their classroom doors to let students in out of the rain earlier than the scheduled class time, as it was almost impossible for the assistant principal and me to supervise the students alone. Immediately the union person at my school called to complain about the rainy day schedule plan. The idea was dropped.] The union is always ruining our plans here at the school.

Ms. H: [I'm sure that my two highly vocal teachers active in the local teachers' association keep the school from moving forward.] They don't come to me with problems but go to the superintendent; the new superintendent lets that happen. That has become the mode of operation in this school and it's difficult to operate in that environment.

We found that the compelling modesty described by Collins was only partly evidenced in the comments made by the comparison principals. Like the highly successful principals, most comparison principals gave credit to others. However, they were quick to pass on blame for efforts that were not successful. Not one highly successful principal blamed the teachers' union or others for failures at the school.

REFLECTION

Think of a school principal you know. How does she or he exude compelling modesty? How is this quality important given her or his present work? When might "just plain luck" be an appropriate answer to why something successful happens?

SUGGESTIONS FOR PRINCIPALS

Exhibiting Compelling Modesty

- Downplay being *I*-centric and charismatic.
- Assign credit to others for success.
- Acknowledge the work of teachers as the reason for improved student performance.
- Minimize the part you play.

Accepting the Blame

- Accept blame for failures.
- At times, assign personal success to "luck."

5

Be Ambitious First for the School's Success

Great ambition is the passion of a great character. Those endowed with it may perform very good or very bad acts. All depends on the principles which direct them.

—Napoleon I, French emperor (1769–1821)

Ambition, after all, is a healthy sentiment, is it not? The word *ambition* shares a root with the Latin verb *ambire*, "to go around," and is defined as "the act of soliciting for votes" (*Merriam-Webster's*, 2003, p. 39). That word was first used in the fourteenth century, when politicians would travel from place to place to get votes and support. Ambition is not a single-minded focus, a career fixation, or unbridled promotion of oneself at the expense of others. Taken literally and used correctly (although that rarely occurs), to have ambition is to create one's life journey. True ambition is an admirable characteristic—one that the Level 5 Executives in the Collins (2001) study exhibited in wanting to see their company even more successful after they are gone. Collins spoke about David Maxwell, CEO of Fannie Mae, who turned the company over to an equally capable successor. He felt that the company would be ill served if he stayed on too long. Collins quotes one Level 5 Executive as saying, "I want to look out from my porch at one of the great companies in the world someday and be able to say, 'I used to work there'" (p. 26).

AMBITION FOR THE SUCCESS OF THE SCHOOL IS KEY

The key, then, is not whether a person exhibits ambition, but whether his or her ambitions are for self-endorsement or for the success of a greater cause. We set out to find out what the ambitions of our highly successful principals were. Were they more concerned for the success of their schools in improving student performance than they were for their own self-promotion?

In our interviews, the evidence for this characteristic often surfaced in responses to questions about hope principals had for the school if they should leave. For these questions, the highly successful principals' responses indicated their ambitions for the success of the school much more often than the comparison principals did. Examples of highly successful principal responses included the following from Ms. Persevere and Mr. Focus:

Ms. P: I want the passion and the quality of instruction to continue and to even improve. I have heard good things so far. That's what I'm doing this all for.

Mr. F: I want to be remembered for having positive relationships with many people, from which we got many successes. I worked hard to build that climate and believe it will stay if I should leave.

Consider the story of Ms. Aspiration and Mission Elementary School. Her ambitions for the school, combined with her fierce professional will and competitive nature, drove her actions.

MS. ASPIRATION AND MISSION ELEMENTARY SCHOOL

Mission Elementary is a little school situated on a cul-de-sac in a quiet California housing development. The school has been called a secret jewel, partly because of its location and partly because of the reputation it has earned as a Distinguished School, with high student achievement results on the state-mandated assessments (Table 5.1).

Table 5.1   Mission Elementary School: API Similar Schools Rank

1999	2000	2001	2002	2003	2004	2005
8	4	10	10	10	10	9

Mission Elementary made a remarkable jump in Academic Performance Index (API) similar schools rank from a decile of 4 in 2000 to 10 in 2001. Equally impressive was its continuing similar schools rank of 9 or 10 through 2005 and two years after Ms. Aspiration transferred to a different school.

The school serves a typical California mix of students. Approximately 57% of the students are Hispanic (a growing population within the school), 26% are white, 7% are African American, and 5% are Pacific Islander. Thirty percent of the student population are English language learners, most of whom speak Spanish. Fifty-two percent of the students qualify for free or reduced price meals. Mission Elementary is designated schoolwide Title I. Some of the families live in single-family dwellings within walking distance of the school, while others live in apartments in an adjoining valley. These latter children are bused to and from school.

The school has a long history of having a proactive parent organization and, in fact, the entire community that surrounds the school has been very involved. On any given day, many parent and community volunteers are seen coming and going at the school. Open house events are always crowded.

On the surface, the school appeared to be a nice place for children to be. However, there were concerns on the part of the district administration over the growing complacency of the staff. Evidence for that were test scores that were not improving. The current principal had been there for a number of years and was very popular with many of the staff members. Something needed to be done to stir things up. A decision was made to transfer the principal to another school in the district. Shortly thereafter, Ms. Aspiration arrived.

When we arrived at the school, we waited for a few minutes while the principal finished with a meeting she was having with a team of teachers. Through the office walls, we could hear lively discussion, led mainly by questions and comments of the principal, but with a definite collaborative tone. We later learned that the purpose of this meeting was to plan next steps for the cognitive guided instruction (CGI) mathematics program currently being implemented at the school. When the meeting broke up, a group of talkative, energetic teachers emerged from the office of the principal. Trailing behind them was Ms. Aspiration. Her parting comment to the teachers was, "You guys think about it. We'll bring it up with everyone at the staff meeting next week."

Given that initial glimpse of some of the teaching staff and the principal, we were especially eager to understand just what the arrival of Ms. Aspiration on the scene had to do with the remarkable change that took place from 1999 through 2003, which was still present at Mission Elementary School. The interview began by us asking for an overview of how she came to be principal of the school.

Ms. A: There was a big change. The old principal was transferred to a new school. I think I was again brought in to be "Hatchet Woman." The district wanted me to shake things up.

Q: Tell me a little about the staff of Mission Elementary and how they have evolved in the past five years.

Ms. A: When the old principal left, he took most of the staff with him. That meant I could bring in new people to fill those teaching positions. This created a problem in one way, and opened up many doors the other way. For those new teachers, some of whom I selected from my old school, the changes we needed to make were easier and faster. However, lots of staff development was needed and I could see that uniting this new staff with the old staff was not going to be easy. There was no way we were going to improve test scores unless we did that. I didn't care about how hard this was going to be. I just wanted to see the school improve.

Now that the tasks were identified, we were interested in understanding how successful Ms. Aspiration and her staff were in confronting these challenges.

Q: What happened? What decisions did the school make to spur an increase in student achievement prior to receiving a ranking of 10 on the 2001 API?

Ms. A: The scores. I think teachers thought students were doing better than they were. Teachers thought this was a good school. When they saw the ranking of 4 in API, improvement became a goal. In the beginning, it was difficult to get the staff to work together.

Ms. Aspiration went on to share problems she confronted with association people.

Ms. A: The power of the [teachers'] association was strong here. Staff meetings were difficult. In fact, once I had to say to an association teacher, "You need to put away your magazine" during the meeting. Teachers at this school hadn't been made to do much. The old principal had a philosophy of "Everyone is wonderful; everyone is great." The teacher attitude at the school was generally, "Don't touch me. I can do what I want when I want and how I want."

As the interview progressed, we began to hear evidence of what she felt needed to be done in order to move forward.

Q: You mentioned that one of your challenges was to unite your staff. Talk to me more about how you were able to accomplish that.

Ms. A: That meeting you saw me come out of before our interview is an example of things we are doing now. I knew we could raise test scores. I also knew we couldn't do that if we didn't work together. I figured that if we could find something that was important to everyone, the staff would unite itself. Everyone teaches math, so involvement in CGI math became the catalyst for bringing teachers together. We found ourselves with a united goal and everyone went through training.

Ms. Aspiration shared enthusiastically how the staff of Mission Elementary rallied around their mutual goal.

Ms. A: It was a snowball effect. Two teachers would be excited about something going on in math, and soon others would join in. What began to happen is the conversations in the lounge changed from complaining and moaning to "Guess what I did in math today!" Once we got going with CGI, I brought in the notion that what we are teaching should be correlated to the test we are accountable for. We began . . . to raise math scores and then this energy moved into reading. It was exciting to see the school being so successful.

Teachers began assessing students on skills and addressing those skills that were not being learned. Ms. Aspiration and her staff were learning to work together for what is good for students. It was not necessarily just for the test scores. For the five years Ms. Aspiration was principal of Mission Elementary, the staff stayed fairly stable. The training they received was implemented over a longer period. Ms. Aspiration did not move teachers around in grade levels, allowing teachers at each grade level to develop into cohesive teams and focus their attention on what they all agreed were their goals for improving student performance.

Ms. Aspiration's enthusiasm, along with her aspirations for a successful school, laced with a hint of humility, came together full force when asked about her leadership style.

Ms. A: I was a cheerleader in high school so I can say that I am very energetic. At this school, it means I'm in rooms a lot. I try to support
teachers a lot. I've never forgotten that I was a teacher. I came with
a strong background in curriculum knowledge so I know what a
school should look like and what a school would be without a
strong curriculum base. I came to a school that, although they
didn't know it at the time, was ready to learn that stuff. Bringing
in new teachers when I did helped because they were eager to
make a good school.

It was clear that Ms. Aspiration's competitive spirit often drove her
actions. During the next portion of the interview, we talked about what
might happen after she leaves. She never claimed that she was the reason
for something happening. Instead, she would talk about what she wanted
and how "*we* got there."

Ms. A: It really bugged us when a neighboring school got better test scores
or beat us in a local math competition. It just made us want to work
harder. I wanted Mission Elementary to be a Distinguished School
and we got there. My supervisor said, "Don't go yet. Stay there and
enjoy the laurels." I don't need that. It's okay to just say I was part
of it all.

As in the case with all of the highly successful principals, Ms. Aspiration
demonstrated her belief that principal presence in classrooms and elsewhere in the school was critical for improving instruction and increasing
student achievement.

Q: What did you do to ensure that teachers continued to focus on
improving student performance? How did you know teachers
were implementing CGI?

Ms. A: I was in the classrooms often observing lessons and giving teachers
feedback about what I saw. I listened and got them the resources
they needed. I made sure teachers met as a team and had agendas
for their meetings. I made sure they had targets for improvement.
I met with every student to talk about test scores. I made sure we
celebrated incremental growth.

Ms. Aspiration readily admitted that she used the pressures of district,
state, and federal accountability as a mechanism for needed change, just as
she used the demands of the community and the knowledge that many of
the teachers at her school were new to teaching.

Ms. A: I used [mandated test] scores as a catalyst. The state and its testing program was my scapegoat. The community of this school is
demanding and the test scores are going to be in the newspaper

for everyone to see. Many of my staff were new and didn't know anything more than that they needed to improve their instruction.

The interview ended with this question and Ms. Aspiration's heartfelt response.

Q: What else would you like to tell me about the reasons for the success of your school in raising student performance?

Ms. A: When I look back, I think, Wow! I am so proud of being a part of that school. They really performed. Should I have stayed there? We were on a roll. Maybe I should have stayed there . . . or maybe it was the time to move. I have always been of the opinion that change is good.

After five years at Mission Elementary, Ms. Aspiration accepted an opportunity to transfer to another school principalship in the district, where she continues today. She contemplates whether the Mission Elementary teachers' attitudes will change and they will revert to complacency now that she is not there to energize them. She will always wonder if, had she been given more time, Mission Elementary would have received that Blue Ribbon Award.

HIGHLY SUCCESSFUL PRINCIPALS AND AMBITION FOR THE SCHOOL'S SUCCESS

The highly successful principals provided evidence in their interviews that they promoted professionalism and leadership in their staff to further the success of the school. Mr. Unpretentious involved all of his teachers in leadership team training and continued to promote leadership by including every teacher in some aspect of decision making for the school. He does not expect this will change when he leaves.

Mr. U: The staff will be the same staff and they are still going to work together whether I am there or not.

Ms. Persevere had her star teachers, whom she coached and trained to take a leadership role in implementing programs at the school. She hopes that this core of star teachers will sustain the positive trend of the school.

Ms. P: I want the passion and the quality of instruction to continue and to even improve. I have heard good things so far.

Both Mr. Bond and Mr. Focus exhibited their ambition for the success of their schools, as well as their modesty and personal humility, when asked what their hopes were for the school should they leave.

Mr. B: When you are a referee for a sport like basketball, and there is silence as you walk off the court, you know you are doing a good job. Don't expect someone to come up and congratulate you for a job well done. Silence is my way of knowing that what I do and what I have done here made a difference in the success of this school. This school will be okay when I leave and another principal takes my place.

Mr. F: I want the school to keep moving forward. It has a very strong foundation and I want things to continue with the successes they have already had. I feel proud that I was part of it all.

COMPARISON PRINCIPALS AND AMBITION FOR THE SCHOOL'S SUCCESS

Responses from Ms. Ineffectual and Ms. Oblivious reflected their hopes for the continued success of their schools.

Ms. I: I think I'm most proud that I can leave the school with teachers who are knowledgeable and who want to continue the work we have started.

Ms. O: I'm most proud when I go into classrooms and see exciting things going on; when I see kids are comfortable, know parents like the school, and teachers stay. I feel good about that and about the part I played in all of it.

Comments by the comparison principals such as those above, however, were more often an afterthought at the end of our interview with them. Their statements bore little connection to information we gleaned from earlier responses suggestive of a dearth of professional will and unwavering resolve. Ms. Relinquish also expressed her ambitions for her school.

Q: What do you want most for your school?

Ms. R: I would like to think that I created Johnson Elementary to be a strong and great school and the students have learned something and that would continue whether I'm here or not.

In contrast to her comment above, Ms. Relinquish shared earlier in her interview the barriers she had experienced because of a strong union influence, in which a small number of her teachers were members. Her reaction to these barriers was to stand aside and allow these teachers to make decisions for her school that were not always in the best interest of her school.

We are drawn back to the quote by Napoleon at the beginning of this chapter: "Great ambition is the passion of a great character. . . . All depends on the principles which direct them." The ambitions the highly successful principals had for their school in increasing student performance were clear throughout our conversations, whether they were referring to staffing decisions or prioritizing activities and programs.

REFLECTION

Assume that you are a successful principal who has just learned that you are being transferred to another school. How might you assist your successor in ensuring that student performance continues to improve at the school from which you are departing?

SUGGESTIONS FOR PRINCIPALS

Exercising Ambition for the School Before Ambition for Self

- Strive to see the school even more successful after you are gone.
- Encourage professionalism and leadership among staff.
- Value staff development.
- Offer assistance to your successor.

Promoting Competitive Staff

- Promote competitive spirit for the whole school.
- Select staff who are eager to see that the school is successful and willing to do whatever it takes to make that success happen.

6

Resolve to Do What Needs Doing . . . Then Do It!

Nothing in the world can take the place of Persistence. Talent will not; nothing is more common than unsuccessful men with talent. Genius will not; unrewarded genius is almost a proverb. Education will not; the world is full of educated derelicts. Persistence and determination alone are omnipotent. The slogan "Press on" has solved and always will solve the problems of the human race.

—Calvin Coolidge, 30th president of the United States (1872–1933)

When veteran teachers who need to attend staff development refuse to do so, what can you do? If teachers are not on board with decisions made, what can you do? We believe what we read in the literature written about effective leadership, so our research finding, and the subject of this chapter, came as no surprise to us. Successful leaders have fierce resolve and an enduring determination. Successful leaders identified in Collins' (2001) study were determined to get what they wanted, when they wanted it. Unwavering resolve takes professional will to a fervent level of fierce resolve or stoic determination to do whatever needs to be done to make the company great. Private sector leaders with unwavering resolve adopt what Collins described as a "workmanlike diligence—more plow horse than show horse . . . fanatically driven, infested with an incurable need to produce results" (p. 30).

APPLICATION OF UNWAVERING RESOLVE TO SCHOOLS

We found it easy to understand why CEOs in the private sector would be fanatically driven to produce profits, but we wondered just how school leaders would be so driven. A 1996 study involving 491 outstanding administrators gave us a clue. The study reported that these effective school administrators illustrated their professional will through their determination, commitment, and resolve to do what needs to be done (Wendel, Hoke, & Joekel, 1996). To speak to this topic of resolve, we asked many questions of all our principals, focusing on factors that led to their school's success in improving student performance and the part, if any, the principals themselves played in this effort. All of the highly successful principals in our study displayed an enduring resolve in their descriptions of staff interactions and in meeting the challenges of improving student learning at their schools. First, we look at the fierce resolve of Ms. Persevere.

MS. PERSEVERE AND MOUNTAIN HIGH ELEMENTARY SCHOOL

Mountain High Elementary School initially earned its status as highly successful because of its high California Academic Performance Index (API) rankings during the period from 1999 through 2003. The school has continued since then to earn high marks, both in relative ranking and in similar schools ranking (Table 6.1).

This California school has served its community for more than 50 years. Of the approximately 450 kindergarten through fifth-grade students attending, about 48% of the students are white, 25% are Hispanic, 6% are African American, and 21% are other. Fifteen percent of the students are English language learners, and 28% of the students qualify for free or reduced price

Table 6.1   Mountain High Elementary School: API Relative Rank
and Similar Schools Rank

	1999	2000	2001	2002	2003	2004	2005
Relative Rank	8	8	8	9	8	9	8
Similar Schools Rank	8	10	9	9	10	10	10

meals. The enrollment at Mountain High Elementary is declining, as are enrollments of many of the schools in the area. Most of the families are lower middle class to middle class, with a number of children of poverty whose families live in local mobile home parks and hotels. The mobility rate for students is relatively high, especially for those students who live in hotels. While the student population is mobile, teachers at the school are not. Leadership was needed to rekindle the enthusiasm of these veteran teachers. Test scores were considered decent, especially by the teachers who did not have high expectations for a student population characterized by these demographics. They were content to let things be at Mountain High Elementary. Why try to fix a school that isn't really broken?

It was late in the day as we approached the front offices of Mountain High Elementary School. Darkness had set in and we thought that most people would already be gone. However, when we opened the doors of the school office, the scene was anything but deserted. The school secretary was on the phone, parents were chatting with students, and a teacher was pinning an announcement for her class theater production on the large, brightly decorated bulletin board next to the entrance of the office. We heard Ms. Persevere before we saw her. As she rounded the corner of the hallway, we could just make out her comment to the teacher walking with her, "If she doesn't agree with you, let me know. I'll talk with her. Everybody has to be on board for this to work." We wondered what this comment was all about and made a note to ask Ms. Persevere about it later.

Ms. Persevere was known as a mover and a shaker even before she became a school principal. She had spent the first 10 years of her educational career as an elementary teacher, and then moved to a position as a science and technology resource teacher. The district superintendent was impressed with the work she was already doing for the district, thinking she was exactly the type of personality needed to lead this school from good to great. Before long, she was hired as principal of Mountain High Elementary School and was ensured of a tough, uphill battle ahead. In many ways, this was to be her proving ground.

Our first questions for Ms. Persevere were about the staff at her school and how they had evolved. It was clear from the beginning, regardless of preexisting issues at the school, that this principal had unwavering resolve to do whatever needed doing and that she did it without backing down one inch.

Ms. P: The principals that came before me here stayed here until they retired. When I inherited the school, I was directed by the superintendent to light a fire under the teachers. They were very set in their ways. They lacked passion and were rather stale.

Ms. Persevere had been a staff developer in the district for years before coming to the school and was surprised that she knew none of the teachers. She did not recognize any of the staff at this school because they never attended any of the district trainings. Well, it was a veteran staff. They did not go to staff development because they didn't think they needed to. They thought test scores at their school were good enough. Ms. Persevere was determined to turn that attitude around. However, she also knew that she needed to be patient. She felt she should first become part of the school's culture before trying to change that culture.

Q: What did you do to get things moving?

Ms. P: To be blunt, some of the teachers needed to find a new career. However, because this was my first year at the school—not to mention my first year as a principal anywhere—I made very subtle changes, [first] establishing rapport, gaining trust, and being supportive. I'd say things like, "You guys are the best thing since sliced bread!" I'm really good at schmoozing.[1]

In the meantime, I learned everything I could about each of the teachers, their classroom programs, and the schoolwide programs. By the middle of that first year, I was able to put into place some programs that were so badly needed that some of the teachers, who recognized and accepted that things needed to change, really appreciated it. However, some teachers who were at risk became very nervous.

The conversation with Ms. Persevere continued with a question about what she observed when she visited classrooms. She expressed her concerns that full implementation of the district program of guided reading was not in evidence in every classroom.[2]

---

1. Schmoozing as a means of persuasion surfaced among several of the highly successful principals during their interviews. "To schmooze" means "to chat in a friendly and persuasive manner especially to gain favor, business, or connections" (*Merriam-Webster's*, 2003, p. 1,111).

2. Fountas and Pinnell (1996) define guided reading as "a context in which a teacher supports each reader's development of effective strategies for processing novel texts at increasingly challenging levels of difficulty. The teacher works with a small group of children who use similar reading processes and are able to read similar levels of text with support" (p. 2).

Ms. P: My main concern had to do with the district mandate at that time that teachers teach guided reading five days a week. The teachers here were not doing that and, to me, that was a big issue and the reason that test scores were not continuing to go up.

Q: How did you deal with that?

Ms. P: The primary teachers were ready for change and could see the positive side to guided reading five days a week. I began working with them, giving them lots of support. Some of these teachers really blossomed and became stars. They really were passionate about improving student performance but the expectation just had not been there to spur them on.

As the interview progressed, Ms. Persevere's responses confirmed that her resolve is a force to be reckoned with.

Q: While you were working with the primary teachers, what were upper-grade teachers thinking?

Ms. P: Some of the upper-grade teachers were very stubborn and it was clear that they were not going to adjust to change easily. I called two of the key problem teachers in and gently prepared them to get ready [to] teach guided reading every day of the week beginning in the fall of the next school year. I showed them the data. Their test scores were erratic. I found that I did not need to say much. I wasn't rough with them. With teachers, data speaks for itself.

This principal also put her persistence to good use in ensuring that she got the right people to replace teachers who didn't work out.

Ms. P: If I find that a teacher is at risk and have a concern, I get 100% support from the district in dealing with that teacher, whether a transfer is in order or I need to write the teacher up. The district screens teacher applicants and then I can go down and pick the teacher I feel is best for the school.

Q: And, if teachers want to transfer into your school?

Ms. P: Even if three teachers wanted to transfer in for one position, I have the final call as far as which one would be a fit for the school. I do what I need to do to be certain that happens.

Ms. Persevere did not let up on her hedgehog-like expectation that student performance could and should improve. She never deviated from that focus and did things to ensure the staff did not either. One tactic she used was to build a positive relationship between her and each of the teachers, and among the teachers to entice them to take collective action. She developed trust through persistently modeling her own teaching skills and supporting teachers with the resources they needed to be successful.

She did all these things consciously. She wanted to hook key teachers into supporting what she was asking them to do. She knew she could never ask them to do something that she could not do herself.

Ms. P: Since teachers from this school did not go to district trainings, I went to the trainings instead and came back to train them myself. I also provided them with release time for coaching, looking at data, and professional development.

Ms. Persevere was adamant that there be no barriers to incorporating guided reading strategies every day. Her resolve was clear as she shared how she dealt with reticent teachers.

Ms. P: Remember, I required all of the upper-grade teachers to teach guided reading five days a week beginning in the second year. A couple of the teachers said it was a good idea but that it required too much preparation. I prepared all of the materials for them, so they had no excuse. I was relentless. If a teacher said, "This program is not working for me," I'd say, "Can I come in and teach it?" I was obstinate. I just would not let them not do it. I feel the same today.

Collins (2001) referred to the use of technology as an accelerator as one of the attributes of a successful leader. We found that our highly successful principals and their staffs made decisions about technology in the same way they made decisions about any program or action in their school. If it did not fit their hedgehog concept of student performance results, they didn't do it. Ms. Persevere commented often that she and her staff never deviated from the focus of getting student performance results. She was a zealot in ensuring that nothing kept them from that focus.

Q: You've talked a lot about not deviating from the focus. Can you give me an example of an action or decision made or not made by the school that demonstrates that focus?

Ms. P: Someone on the staff had the idea of purchasing some language arts enrichment software for our computer lab with the money [funds awarded by the State of California to the school for improved test scores]. The staff decided against that because the research on that particular software didn't convince us that using it improved student performance in reading. Instead, we purchased laptops for every teacher. We also spent funds to see that they had training in using the laptops, both for record keeping and for instructional purposes. I began to see teachers adding sparkle to their reading instruction using these laptops.

Everything Ms. Persevere did was calculated to promote the needed changes at her school. She was relentless in making decisions and carrying out actions that focused on student performance results. However, as Ms. Persevere indicates, there wasn't any one decision or action made by either her or her staff that provided the momentum for improvement in student performance at Mountain High Elementary School. By the end of the second year of her principalship, tornadoes were touching down all over, shaking apart old notions about how things should be done at the school.

Ms. P: The change sure didn't happen overnight, but by the second year things picked up. We all began to realize that the more focused curriculum and the more motivating instructional strategies teachers were using were making a difference in student achievement. We were taking baby steps. I could just feel it when I was pushing them too fast. I'd back off. After a couple of years of keeping to our focus on results in reading, all of a sudden things took off. In some ways, it was magical.

Collins (2001) found indications that some of the leaders in his study had significant life experiences that might have helped shape their leadership. Other leaders in the study, however, had no obvious experience; they just led ordinary lives and somehow ended up as successful CEOs. Similarly, we wanted to see whether there were life experiences that fostered successful leadership in our principals. We asked the same question used by Collins and his research team during interviews with CEOs. The responses of Ms. Persevere confirmed she had, in fact, had things happen to her in the past that were now reflected in her unwavering resolve.

Ms. P: I'm a survivor. We were very poor. I was a single parent. My son battles with serious diabetes. I struggled with issues within my family that have strengthened my character and toughened me up.

Even in her responses to questions about her leadership style, Ms. Persevere exuded unwavering resolve.

Q: What kind of leadership style do you think you have?

Ms. P: I would call myself "deliberate." I rarely make decisions without having buy-in from the staff even though it would save a lot of time if I did. I know better.

Ms. Persevere is relentless in making certain that the momentum of increasing student performance continues.

Ms. P: I'm in classrooms all the time. I want to be part of the classroom furniture. If I don't see the program that we have all agreed to,

I confront the teacher. If the teacher refuses to do what the team has agreed to do, a rare occasion, I won't hesitate to turn to the district's employee disciplinary process. On the other hand, I want to be a resource to teachers. I'll help them prepare their lessons or teach the lesson if necessary.

Without asking, we think we know what that comment we heard from Ms. Persevere as she rounded the corner in the office before our interview began was in reference to.

Ms. Persevere has since moved on to work with another school in the district. She believed the quality of instruction will continue to improve at Mountain High Elementary because of the staff's relentless focus on student performance results. She was confident that her star teachers will carry on serving as role models for others at the school. During her tenure at Mountain High Elementary School, Ms. Persevere understood what needed doing and accomplished it with resolve. This is what highly successful school principals do.

COMPARISON PRINCIPALS AND RESOLVE

The principals in the comparison group all shared their initial resolve to be a positive influence in moving their schools forward. Ms. Conspiracy came closest to accomplishing her resolve when she insisted that teachers implement a program employing direct instruction as the primary instructional strategy in their classes. She provided staff development for every teacher and offered them opportunities to observe the program being implemented in a classroom. When some teachers refused to take advantage of observing in a classroom, she brought students to a regularly scheduled staff meeting and demonstrated the instruction to them that way. However, like other comparison principals, Ms. Conspiracy at some point resigned herself to the difficulties that the power of the teachers' union presented to her and her staff.

Ms. C: We went through two years of hell dealing with the union. I've tried everything I could think of to fix it. Now what?

Ms. Relinquish's resolve to open classroom doors to let children in out of the rain before class time has succumbed to the requirements of the teacher contract.

Ms. R: The union makes my job very difficult in that they believe that they are running the school by contract. Teachers are duty free here, thanks to the superintendent who "gave that to the union." How are we going to cover the classrooms on rainy day if teachers don't stay with their kids?

Ms. Oblivious spoke of the lack of parent involvement when asked how her school gets commitment and agreement with its decisions from them.

She seemed resigned to this missing piece of the student achievement puzzle at her school.

Ms. O: Parents aren't involved and haven't been as long as I've been here. They are happy with the way things are going at the school. The expectation of our parents is that schools know what they are doing and it's not their place to tell us how to run the school. I know I should do something to get them more involved. My efforts so far have been a waste of my time.

As we noted at the top of this chapter, Calvin Coolidge said, "The slogan 'Press on' has solved and always will solve the problems of the human race." The resolve to make a difference for most comparison principals was curtailed often by frustrating and seemingly endless personnel-related issues. In contrast, the highly successful principals we interviewed were relentless in their determination to press on in meeting the mission and vision of the school, regardless of hurdles that confronted them.

REFLECTION

Think about a time in your life when you resolved to do something. What requisites need to be in place in order to maintain unwavering resolve?

SUGGESTIONS FOR PRINCIPALS

Exhibiting Unwavering Resolve

- Be relentless and aggressive in working toward the mission and vision of the school.
- Be continuously involved with the primary operations of the school through committee work, classroom visitations, grade-level meetings, or department meetings.

Communicating the Resolve to Staff

- Be persuasive.
- Maintain and communicate the belief that something can and will be accomplished.
- Communicate clarity of purpose: a clear goal should be in sight at all times.
- Accept no excuses.

7

Get the Right People on the Bus

Lots of people want to ride with you in the limo, but what you want is someone who will take the bus with you when the limo breaks down.

—Oprah Winfrey, entertainer (1954–)

Collins (2001) found that the Level 5 Executives first got the right people on the bus, the wrong people off the bus, and the right people in the right seats, and only then did they figure out where to drive the bus. CEOs of corporations studied by Collins did not need to ask permission to personally fire, demote, or reassign personnel who were not right for the organization. They just did it. In this way, they could take disciplined action within a system designed around the hedgehog concept. Because they got the right people on the bus and the wrong people off the bus, these leaders did not spend any time motivating or convincing their team to move forward. "The old adage 'People are your most important asset' turns out to be wrong. People are not your most important asset. The *right* people are" (p. 13).

> The *Good to Great* companies built a consistent system with clear constraints, but they also gave people freedom and responsibility within the framework of that system. They hired self-disciplined people who didn't need to be managed, and then managed the systems, not the people. (p. 125)

Sergiovanni (1992) defined these right people as having the quality of professionalism that can substitute for leadership: "Professionals don't need anybody to check on them, to push them, to lead them. They are compelled from within" (p. 46).

Louis and Miles (1990), during the course of their case studies of five urban high schools that were engaged in major improvement projects, found getting the people first and then deciding what to do next was the smart way to proceed. They observed, "The more successful of our schools had no a priori mission statements. Instead, multiple improvement efforts coalesced around a theme or set of themes only after the activity had begun" (p. 206). Max De Pree (1989), former chairman of Herman Miller, demonstrated the importance he placed on "getting the right people on the bus" when he assumed the following: "The best people working for organizations are like volunteers. Since they could probably find good jobs in any number of groups, they choose to work somewhere for reasons less tangible than salary or position" (p. 28) such as "shared commitment to ideas, to issues, to values, to goals, and to management process" (p. 60).

SCHOOL LEADERS' DIFFICULTIES IN GETTING THE RIGHT PEOPLE

One difference between the business environment and the educational environment is that school principals do not often have the luxury of getting the wrong people off the bus while getting the right people on the bus. State law, labor agreements, and board regulations make firing personnel at the school level difficult—especially when the cause for dismissal is a lack of shared commitment or some other subjective reason. (Differences between the auton-omy of principals and the autonomy of private sector leaders are discussed in more detail in Chapter 11.) The few cases where principals often do have the power to hire and fire personnel occur when they are brought in to quickly fix a school in trouble, or to set up a specialized or charter school. Principals of standard good schools do not usually have that autonomy. When asked how one can practice the discipline of the "right people on the bus and the wrong people off the bus" in schools, Collins (2005) responds by saying that this continues to apply, but that tenure and other such conditions of public education pose challenges that may result in this practice requiring more effort to accomplish (p. 14). Yes, you might have to carry the wrong people along for the time being. Researchers in educational leadership have argued that controlling staff hiring and development practices is a variable for success in creating an effective school community, and that one of the conditions linking leadership to strong schools is site administrator auton-omy (Coleman et al., 1966; Purkey & Smith, 1983; Teske & Schneider, 1999). In a study of Chicago schools (DeMoss, 2002), one leader considered effec-tive because of improved student performance in his school was adept at helping teachers who did not fit his vision to transfer to other schools. He had built a cadre of teachers dedicated to their school's instructional pro-gram just as our highly successful principals did.

AN EXAMPLE OF GETTING THE RIGHT PEOPLE

Collins (2005) shared a story of a high school physics teacher, Roger Briggs, in Boulder, Colorado. Briggs set out to improve his science department by getting seriously involved in the process for hiring excellent teachers to fill vacated positions in his department. He was determined that adequate was not an acceptable accomplishment for his teachers. He began by telling new teachers in his department that they most likely would not receive tenure unless they proved themselves as exceptional teachers. Then, when an "only adequate" probationary teacher came up for tenure, Briggs argued against tenure and held firm and the teacher received noti-fication that he was not to be rehired. There was no recourse for the teacher. With a position vacant, a new, excellent teacher could be brought on board. "The science department minibus changed—hire by hire and tenure decision by tenure decision—until a critical mass coalesced into a culture of discipline" (p. 14). Here was a case where a leader, who was not the principal, superintendent, or governor was still able to get the right people on the bus.

If a science teacher could do it, given many restraints, a school principal can most certainly do it. As we have observed, while principals can reassign teachers to different grade levels, they do not normally have the autonomy to hire and fire except through processes regulated by the district.

The principals we interviewed described various processes for hiring, such as the following:

1. A district pool of applicants who meet the high expectations of the district and would be successful at any school in the district is created. In this case, the district may assign the applicants to the schools or the principals may select from the district pool of applicants.

2. Principals get together to interview applicants and then barter with each other to get the teacher they want for their school. This was the process of choice in the districts of four of the six highly successful principals.

3. Once a district pool of teachers is created, applicants have the final word on where they work, which leads principals to sell their school to the teacher applicant. None of the districts of the highly successful principals implemented this hiring process. Two of the districts of the comparison principals used this process.

4. Hiring is accomplished at the school with or without the input of the teaching staff, except in the case where a teacher voluntarily or involuntarily transfers from another school.

HIGHLY SUCCESSFUL PRINCIPALS AND "FIRST WHO . . . THEN WHAT"

Evidence for this ability to first "get the right people" manifested itself in our interviews somewhat differently for school principals, but very much as in the case of science teacher Roger Briggs. Our highly successful principals showed their persistence in getting who they wanted on their staff, and in getting those teachers who did not work with their program to transfer or leave teaching.

Mr. Focus

All but one of the principals in the study came to an existing school with an existing staff. Mr. Focus, who personally hired all of the staff when he opened a new school, had a great opportunity to "get the right people." He understood the importance of Oprah Winfrey's comment that "what you want is someone who will take the bus with you when the limo breaks down."

Q: What latitude did you have as principal to make decisions you had to make?

Mr. F: The superintendent was good with me. I had a great deal of latitude to do what I felt I needed to do. I don't feel that I was restricted at all, as long as I didn't break the law or annoy any parents.

Mr. Focus was asked what process was used at his school to make key decisions. He described a process that was collegial. Also, in his comments about his confidence in decisions made, he suggested that his school had the right people on the bus from the beginning.

Mr. F: Teachers were working side by side with me to make decisions. If they made the decisions without me, there is no doubt that their decisions would look the same as if I did it myself.

Q: What confidence did you have in the decisions at the time they were made, before you knew their outcome?

Mr. F: It was obvious that I had an excellent staff. I felt good about the decisions we were making from the beginning.

The decision-making process Mr. Focus used for selecting teachers pinpoints his own hedgehog-like focus.

Mr. F: When the memo that a new school was going to open came out, teachers from schools across the district who were interested applied to transfer. I talked with each teacher on the list of transfer requests. I shared with them my philosophy and what the challenges of a diverse student population were. The teachers I selected showed they were interested in opening up a new school and working with the students I described. They shared my philosophy.

Q: How did your selections of teachers work out?

Mr. F: Great! They were so easy to work with, because they were professional, they shared my philosophy, were excellent teachers, and did whatever was needed. The teaching staff loved working there and stayed. The only teachers I lost were teachers who moved out of the area. Two of teachers I hired turned out to be marginal and I worked to make them better.

Ms. Aspiration

Ms. Aspiration also had the opportunity to hire a number of staff at the beginning of her tenure at her school. She, too, was able get the right people on the bus from the beginning. When many of the existing staff followed the previous principal to a different school, she hired teachers to take their place. She was able to make changes easier and faster because so many of the staff were new to the profession or were from her previous school and knew the way she worked.

Q: What latitude did you have as principal of the school to hire and fire teachers after you made the initial selections?

Ms. A: Staffing is always a restriction because you have to go through the district process instead of just hiring the one you want. The good news is that I seldom needed new teachers. Once they got here, they stayed.

In the case of most of the highly successful principals, once initial changes in staff were made, their teaching staff was very stable, with few teachers ever leaving the school. When these principals did need to hire staff, they were all aggressive at finessing, politicking, and persuading to get the teachers they wanted for their school. When there was a situation where more than one principal in a district wanted a particular applicant, all of the highly successful principals described successes in using persuasive and persistent methods to get the right person for their school. The highly successful principals also described their persistence or politicking (or both) at the district level—within legal boundaries—to cause the transfer of teachers who did not wish to implement the focus or mission of the school, or who were sabotaging other teachers' efforts. Ms. Persevere's resolve and adeptness in getting rid of teachers who did not agree with her philosophy serves as one more example of these leaders' capacity for making room for the right people.

Ms. Discipline

Ms. Discipline's story was somewhat different from the other highly successful principals. She hired much of the staff of Eagle Elementary School because of changes in the district.

While Ms. Discipline stated that she hired most of the teachers, she did so within the rules and regulations of the district's hiring process. She was, however, aggressive in getting her choices for teachers when she participated with other principals in interviewing applicants.

COMPARISON PRINCIPALS AND "FIRST WHO . . . THEN WHAT"

All of the principals in the study acknowledged the importance of having discretion over the hiring of teachers at their schools and talked about the restrictions they had in dealing with personnel. The comparison principals had different scenarios to share about their take on the personnel procedures in their district. Ms. Ineffectual demonstrated her frustrations in this area.

Ms. I: I think the hardest thing is not truly being able to hire people you want or keep people on your staff that you want. I'm a supporter of the union but sometimes the union contract gets in our way. Seniority sometimes takes positions away from a new teacher. I sat with the union a lot. Sometimes working with the unions about personnel issues takes up hours of my time. Getting a teacher is one thing. Getting rid of a teacher is another thing. I don't want to keep any teachers that don't work well with kids but sometimes getting rid of them is just too hard. Everything I try to do to be sure our teachers are good teachers is stalled by the union.

Q: What do you want most for your school?

Ms. I: I would like for our students to have teachers who care about them, are knowledgeable, who get to know their students and work with them. Not all of my teachers are like that. I can't rejoice at having one super teacher. Children need to have a super teacher every year they are in school.

Comparison principals shared their frustrations over problems they had with teachers, caused in part by restrictions to their hiring and firing authority, as imposed by the district and union contracts. Ms. Helpless was no exception.

Q: What have you tried that didn't work in the past few years?

Ms. H: I tried to do some work with a leadership team. I still have found working with that team a challenge. How do you create teacher leaders unless they are natural leaders? Then there are those teachers who are [isolated] and want to be isolated from other teachers that won't go along with anything. How do I create enough of a group out of the teachers that I'm given that is supportive of everything and will move the school despite the others who pull us in other directions? I can't say I've figured that out.

Staffs at two of the comparison schools were highly mobile for reasons described by principals as beyond their control. Both Ms. Conspiracy and Ms. Helpless shared that teachers at their schools get tenure and then district policy allows them to transfer to the easier schools up the hill or on the east side of their towns where the students come from wealthier families and with fewer barriers to learning. That leaves their schools with new or marginal teachers.

Ms. Conspiracy disclosed her annoyance with her district's process of selling a school to perspective teachers and her own inadequacies in getting the right people on the bus.

Ms. C: Sometimes we don't have the right people for the positions. In this district, if a teacher applicant is wanted by more than one school, [the principals] must "sell" our school like car salesmen to the applicant. Selling isn't my thing so we don't get the exceptional teachers here.

Comparison principals did not reveal that they were able to go the extra mile and use persuasive and persistent methods, as our highly successful principals did, to get the right people for their school.

All of the principals interviewed acknowledged the importance of having effective teachers at their schools. The differences between highly successful principals and comparison principals were in the way in which they worked with their district's hiring procedures. The unwavering resolve and professional will of the highly successful principals worked to their advantage when hiring new teachers. Comparison principals, on the other hand, were more likely to cite examples where they had little or no control over who their teachers were.

REFLECTION

Given present limitations of hiring and firing procedures in your district, what can you do to ensure your school gets the right people on the bus and the wrong people off the bus? Why is it important to get the right people before you decide what needs to be accomplished?

SUGGESTIONS FOR PRINCIPALS

Getting the Right People

- To the maximum degree possible, maintain the latitude to hire and dismiss school staff.
- Be aggressive in your choices for teachers while staying within the rules and regulations of the district's hiring process.
- Clarify your vision with potential faculty from the beginning to foster a fit with school staff.
- Work with district personnel and other principals to refine the hiring process.

Working With the Right People

- Convince the staff who do not work well with the school program to transfer.
- Work with teachers who desire to improve and who have the capacity to improve.

8

Confront the Brutal Facts

A real leader faces the music, even when he doesn't like the tune.

—Anonymous

W e look now to what Collins (2001) termed "confront the brutal facts." His study of successful CEOs found that the Level 5 Executives of *Good to Great* companies maintained firm belief that the company can and will be successful in the end, regardless of the difficulties that they might face. It is a duality best explained by a brief discussion of the story of Admiral Jim Stockdale. He was a prisoner of war at the Hoa Loa ("fiery furnace") Prison, known ironically as the Hanoi Hilton, during the Vietnam War. When Jim Collins himself asked Stockdale how he was able to survive the ordeal, he replied,

> I never lost faith in the end of the story. I never doubted not only that I would get out, but also that I would prevail in the end and turn the experience into the defining event of my life, which, in retrospect, I would not trade. (p. 85)

He was also asked who didn't survive imprisonment. He responded,

> The optimists. Oh, they were the ones who said, "We're going to be out by Christmas." And, Christmas would come and Christmas would go. Then they'd say, "We're going to be out by Easter." And Easter would come and Easter would go. And then Thanksgiving, and then it would be Christmas again. Then they died of a broken heart. (p. 85)

SCHOOLS FACE CHALLENGES

How does confronting the brutal facts play out in schools? Some in the K–12 school community might say that today's school leader has as his or her primary function to provide the necessary vision—and leadership to achieve that vision. We agree with Collins that equally important with providing a vision is creating a climate where the truth is heard and the brutal facts are confronted "even when he doesn't like the tune," as the anonymous wag said. Unless a principal faces the brutal facts, how can an important vision be created?

The list of challenges facing schools today is long. Some of those we read about regularly in newspapers and journals across the country include accountability and the No Child Left Behind Act, the achievement gap between diverse student populations, language barriers, issues with unions and contracts, student discipline, grade inflation, and the shortage of highly qualified teachers. Teachers and principals in schools everywhere can be heard commiserating about students not doing their homework, or parents not being involved in their children's education.

However, there is hope. Mike Schmoker, in his book *Results Now* (2006), advised administrators and teachers to confront the brutal facts of education.

Schmoker encouraged his readers to see the brutal facts as opportunities to "blow the lid off school attainment, dramatically and swiftly reduce the achievement gap, and enhance the 'life chances' of all children, regardless of their social or economic circumstances" (p. 2).

The good news is that principals and teachers in some schools are coming together as a collaborative team to face these challenges and do something about them. As we see it, the brutal facts are the ones ignored by the comparison principals because it would be uncomfortable or inconvenient to acknowledge these facts, let alone struggle with, them. Paul Houston (2006), executive director of the American Association of School Administrators, said in reference to the shortage of highly qualified teachers, "We must get out of the muck and mud by confronting the brutal facts of our existence" (p. 3).

BRUTAL FACTS TACKLED BY THE PRINCIPALS IN OUR STUDY

In Chapter 1, we listened in on a conversation that school administrators were having about how some schools were successful even though they were challenged by difficult barriers of one sort or the other. It turns out that the principals in our study wrestled with many of these barriers. Although there were many more barriers discussed, four major issues in particular dominated large portions of the interview conversation with highly successful principals as well as with comparison principals. These barriers were (1) teacher isolation and lack of teamwork, (2) poor student performance, (3) stagnating classroom instruction, and (4) difficult staff members. The way the highly successful principals dealt with these barriers was very different from the way the comparison principals dealt with them. The issue was not identifying the challenges or barriers, but rather overcoming them.

HIGHLY SUCCESSFUL PRINCIPALS AND CONFRONTING THE BRUTAL FACTS

This behavior showed itself frequently when principals were asked what defining moment or issue caused them to make a change. Examples of statements made in interviews with highly successful principals indicative of confronting the brutal facts include the following from Mr. Bond, Mr. Focus, and Ms. Persevere:

Mr. B: We needed to look at what we should do in order to improve what we were doing in the classroom; the ironic part was we were on the right road. I said to them that it is tough to take, but in the end we get additional funding to continue what we have already started.

Mr. F: We started with a school with over half of the kids below the 20th percentile in reading, so we put our emphasis in reading instruction and creating environments where kids read more.

Ms. P: Teachers were set in their ways with little sparkle in the classrooms. Test scores reflected that. I collected data and that gave me ammunition, so to speak, to make changes.

Mr. Bond

Almost all of the highly successful principals said that at the beginning of their tenure at the school they were faced with difficult challenges that they were convinced they could resolve. Mr. Bond related the staff's reaction to news that student achievement results following the first full year of his tenure were not acceptable. Their reaction reminded us somewhat of those soldiers who shared a prison with Admiral Stockdale in Vietnam who were overly optimistic about being released from prison. When it did not happen when they thought it would, they gave up.

Mr. B: The news from the state was disappointing to everyone. We had actually made improvement over the past year. Teachers were sure we would do well enough to keep out of trouble. [The improvement they made] just was not good enough. At first, not everyone could believe it. Then I heard teachers blaming the state accountability system.

Mr. Bond confronted the brutal fact that the school was underperforming. He turned that information into a positive move for the school by telling his teachers that the state was providing funds for them to develop a plan of action and implement what they had already begun. To do all that, the staff needed to work together effectively, in both the planning phase and the implementation phase. It was then that Mr. Bond confronted what he considered the real barrier to significant student performance improvement at the school. The teachers had a history of going to their own classrooms and closing the doors behind them. Seldom did they work together for any reason. Mr. Bond could see that in order to get higher test scores, he and the staff would need to communicate with each other more and work together to solve these issues.

Q: What was keeping you all from working together?

Mr. B: The teachers seemed defeated. They could easily have been resigned to their fate [of underperforming status] and turned their backs on the work they had already accomplished. We needed to be able to talk about what to do. It was then that I realized that we didn't know how to do that. I mean there was a lack of communication between administration and the teaching staff. It is one of those things where we had to grow together and work together if we wanted to improve.

Mr. Focus

Mr. Focus and his handpicked staff confronted the brutal fact that they had inherited a student population at Pines Elementary School that was weak in reading. To add to that barrier, these same students often came to the school with no language development in any language, and with parents at home who were not able to help. This challenge to a different group of people would have been daunting. We learned that the staff of Pines Elementary shared the principal's philosophy that good reading skills are necessary for success in all areas of academics. The staff and administration agreed from the beginning to focus their efforts on providing opportunities for all Pines Elementary students to read often at school, get homework assistance in an afterschool homework club, and provide a reading program for students at risk entailing a double dose of reading each day by a credentialed teacher. Mr. Focus spoke with conviction:

Mr. F: I knew kids could be taught to read. I knew that kids reading well meant better performance in other subject areas. I also knew that it would take some time to see results. I never for a moment thought the task was impossible. My staff felt the same way.

Pines Elementary School test scores and Triple Crown status (Distinguished Schools Award, Blue Ribbon School Award, and Title I Achievement Award, all within three years) attest to the success of their efforts.

Ms. Persevere

Ms. Persevere believed she could, as a new principal, light a fire under the teaching staff at Mountain View Elementary School. The brutal fact was, however, that the veteran staff was satisfied with things as they were, and saw no need to implement changes. Ms. Persevere was determined to change the attitude of these teachers or assist them in moving on, by transfer, retirement, or change of careers. We examined in detail the steps she took to bring the staff together by her support through modeling, coaching, and providing resources. The changes she made in school processes were subtle the first year, and she spent most of her time gaining their trust and learning about their classrooms. She realized that to get teacher buy-in she would need to be patient but persistent. There were times when she could see changes were coming too fast, and she would slow down. By the end of the first two years, many of the veteran teachers had joined in. Ms. Persevere's persistence and belief that she would succeed in putting the sparkle back in classrooms kept the school moving in a positive direction.

Ms. Aspiration

When Ms. Aspiration arrived at Mission Elementary School, she confronted the brutal fact of a divided teaching staff. She had, on one side, a few highly vocal and aggressive veteran teachers who were also proactive in the teachers' association. On the other side, she had enthusiastic teachers new to the profession and a few teachers who had followed her from her former school. She embraced the fact that she was going to have a tough, uphill battle uniting the staff to meet the goal of improving student performance and had all the confidence in the world that she would succeed. Her initial plan was to have teachers meet during the district-provided minimum days twice a month. From the beginning, she knew this was not going to be easy.

COMPARISON PRINCIPALS AND CONFRONTING THE BRUTAL FACTS

Highly successful principals in this study were able to move their schools forward even when they met head-on with difficult staffs. Comparison principals' ability to cope with the power of the teachers' association at their school was not so apparent.

Ms. Helpless was optimistic in her hopes to build a collaborative culture at her school. Those hopes were dashed by the reality of the difficulties she was having with some of the association people at Elm Elementary School. Her reaction was to resign herself to having no authority.

Q: What latitude do you have as principal of the school to make the decisions you have to make?

Ms. H: We are very much a unionized shop and [are] restricted by the union. The union people are vocal and have quite a bit of power in the district. Some of [the teachers active in the union] love negatives and look for ways to ruin what we are doing here. I used to have an executive officer of the union at my school that was more level headed and would warn me when problems might occur. He transferred to another school. Now what I have is the negative side.

Ms. Helpless could identify the brutal fact that she had difficult staff members at her school.

Ms. H: [The association people at the school] influence others. When others want to do something extra, they are told to not do more than necessary. One of the union people questions every decision I make and does that in front of the whole staff. The frustration is that I do not think he represents the whole staff. Nevertheless, he has so much power through intimidation. It is as though I am trying to lead with one arm behind my back. They are not fighting fair. The rest of the staff is not going to come up against the shadow group. They don't come to me with problems but go straight to the superintendent. It's becoming very difficult to work in that environment. Right now, that is the biggest struggle.

Ms. Helpless feels that the central office does not support her, exacerbating the problems she already has.

Q: Clarify for me what you mean by "that environment."

Ms. H: The new superintendent lets [the union people come straight to the superintendent with problems]. That has become the mode of operation in this school. It is hard when the superintendent gives these people an audience. Then I cannot get a grip on the problem. It's as if they do not want the problem to be solved.

What Ms. Helpless cannot do is believe that through all these challenges she can succeed. She remarked, "My goal is for my teachers to collaborate. But there is this group (the 'shadow group') who wants to stay here, so why try?" She indicated she would probably ask for a transfer to another school or to a central office position.

Ms. Relinquish appeared to have turned decision-making authority at Johnson Elementary School over to the teachers of her school because of the power of the teachers' union. She expressed her frustrations with decision making when she stated, "The union has time allocated at each meeting and by the time they are finished, there isn't time left for my issues. What can I do? I just stand aside."

One of the most dramatic differences between the highly successful principals and the comparison principals was in the way they confronted difficulties and were able to move beyond the difficulties. Again, their unwavering resolve came into play. Some comparison principals shared difficult scenarios where they were not able to deal with difficult teachers and move on. Instead, they resigned themselves to their belief that since these difficult people were not going, their school could not make progress.

REFLECTION

Every school administrator faces some sort of brutal fact or facts that might impede the implementation of the vision he or she has for the school if action is not taken. What are some brutal facts facing schools in your locality and what are you doing about them?

SUGGESTIONS FOR PRINCIPALS

Confronting the Brutal Facts

- With staff, analyze student achievement and demographic data.
- Study the culture of the school and community.

Solving the Dilemmas

- Develop an important vision for the school based on the facts.
- Work through sensitive challenges.
- Have faith that challenges will be overcome and communicate that faith to others.

9

Know What Drives Your Educational Engine and Be Passionate About It

Anything that does not fit with our Hedgehog Concept, we will not do. We will not launch unrelated businesses. We will not make unrelated acquisitions. We will not do unrelated joint ventures. If it doesn't fit, we don't do it. Period.

—Collins (2001, p. 134)

81

As noted in Chapter 1, in his essay *The Hedgehog and the Fox*, Isaiah Berlin (1993) divided people into two basic groups: hedgehogs and foxes. Foxes pursue many ends at the same time and see the world in all its complexity. Hedgehogs, on the other hand, simplify a complex world into one organizing idea, an understanding that unifies and guides everything. For a hedgehog, anything that does not somehow relate to that simple understanding holds no relevance. Researchers found this quality in many top leaders of the private sector. In the late 1970s and early 1980s, the Peters and Waterman ([1982] 2004) study of 75 highly regarded companies showed clearly that these companies had one important attribute in common: they were diligent in keeping things simple in a complex world. Collins applied Berlin's basic ideas to business in his study of *Good to Great* companies. *Good to Great* company leaders center their strategies on (1) what they can be best in the world at, (2) what drives their economic engine, and (3) what they are deeply passionate about. These leaders have a fundamental understanding about the intersection of these three concepts. This intersection Collins dubs the "hedgehog concept."

ACADEMICS TAKE ISSUE

While most academics would accept that knowing what you "can be best at" and "are being deeply passionate" are concepts that could be applied to education, some have taken issue with attempts to apply Collins' (2001) notion of "what drives your economic engine" to schools. After all, public schools—and most other public agencies, for that matter—are not profit-making entities. Collins (2005) himself rethought the notion of economic engine for organizations in the social sector where profit is not the motive. He clumped public schools together with NASA, EPA, the New York Police Department, charter schools, Boys & Girls Clubs, and assorted other public agencies, pointing out that these social sectors depend heavily on both political skill and public support. We would argue that schools are different from other social sector entities in that dependence on personal relationships is even more critical.

OUR TERM: EDUCATIONAL ENGINE

We agree with Collins' (2005) suggestion that the engine for public schools and other social sectors is about human factors. Moreover, we take it a step farther by stating that the engine for schools is driven more by the skill, discipline, willingness, and determination of the principal and staff than by the "time, money, and brand" (p. 18) Collins described for the social sector. We have, because of these differences, adopted the term "educational engine," instead of "economic engine" or "resource engine" to describe this aspect of the hedgehog concept for schools.

When referring to the private sector, Collins (2001) asked, "If you could pick one and only one ratio—profit per x—to systematically increase over time, what x would have the greatest and most sustainable impact on your economic engine?" (p. 104). We ask a modified version of that question in reference to schools: "If you could pick one ratio—student performance per factor x—to systematically increase over time, what factor would have the greatest and most sustainable impact on your educational engine?"

Evidence for this focus on what drives the educational engine in schools appears in the manner in which school personnel attend to student performance objectives. Consider the case of the 90/90/90 schools research conducted in the Milwaukee Public Schools (Reeves, 2000). These schools and others across the nation are acknowledged as exceptional because they are at least 90% combined minority, at least 90% free or reduced price meal qualified students, and at least 90% successful on standardized assessments. The principals and teachers in the 90/90/90 schools win laurels due to their laser-like focus on the educational engine of student achievement, with a particular emphasis on improvement.

In another study, this one of the schools in the Ysleta Independent School District in Texas, Bruce Matsui and his research team (2002) looked for factors that could have accounted for significant improvement of student performance. One significant factor leading to improved student achievement was the school leader's emphasis on reduction of clutter by eliminating programs and projects not specifically aligned with school-based student achievement objectives.

One highly successful principal we interviewed illustrates meeting all three of the tests of the hedgehog concept. Mr. Focus knew what his school is best at doing. He knew what drives the school's educational engine. In addition, he was truly passionate about his school's cause.

MR. FOCUS AND PINES ELEMENTARY SCHOOL

Pines Elementary School is located in California, in a suburban fringe community characterized by old oak trees, flower fields, rolling hills, a golf course, and middle class and semiaffluent homes. The school services a student population that is 53% Hispanic, 36% white, and 4% other. Forty percent of the students are English language learners and 51% of the students qualify for free or reduced price meals. The school's Academic Performance Index (API) relative decile rank increased from 6 to 8 between 1999 and 2003, belying common assumptions about the relationships between poverty, minority enrollment, and student achievement. Moreover, when compared to similar schools, this school has maintained an extraordinary decile rank of 9 or 10 since 1999 (Table 9.1).

Pines Elementary School joins the ranks of the handful of schools in California that have earned Triple Crown status (Distinguished Schools Award, Blue Ribbon School Award, and the Title I Achievement Award), all within three years. These accomplishments beg the question, "Why is this school successful?"

Table 9.1   Pines Elementary School: API Similar Schools Rank

1999	2000	2001	2002	2003	2004	2005
8	9	9	10	10	9	10

In this book thus far, we have taken the position that behind every successful school there is a successful school principal. Pines Elementary School is no exception. Its principal, Mr. Focus, spent his entire educational career in one district. He began as a teacher, then moved to the central office as coordinator of K–12 curriculum, and was quickly elevated to the position of elementary principal. When Mr. Focus had been a principal for seven years, news came across his desk that a new school in the district was slated to open. He requested and received permission to move to the principalship at the new school, Pines Elementary School, where he remained for the next six years. The story of his highly successful career at that school exemplifies the hedgehog concept in educational leadership.

Know What You Are Best At

A company may know what it is best at. Walgreens, one of the *Good to Great* companies highlighted in the Collins (2001) study, discovered a long time ago that if it locates its stores to provide easy access to service, its profits go up. Another *Good to Great* company, Abbott Laboratories, developed a cost-effective health-care system that no other company could replicate. In schools, what you are best at is not so much one product or service, but a combination of human factors. Such was the case with Mr. Focus and Pines Elementary. He got the right people on the bus, and he knew from the start what his school was best at doing.

Q: Tell me a little about the staff of the school and how they have evolved in the past five years.

Mr. F: The teachers showed a genuine interest in opening a new school. They understood what the challenges would be with the student population and looked forward to working with the students.

From the beginning, Mr. Focus saw the school as rich with the raw material— the skill and determination of the teaching staff—needed to realize the potential of all students to be successful academically.

Q: What was the staff like?

Mr. F: The new staff was flexible and focused. They wanted students to be successful. Over the following six years, the staff became close, working together in a positive, collegial, and sharing way. From the beginning, they worked together to find solutions to the challenges that the students of the school presented and were willing to put in the time that it takes to deal with those challenges.

Know What Drives Your Educational Engine

Mr. Focus' responses to our interview questions reflect an answer to the question we asked earlier: "If you could pick one factor—student performance per factor x—to systematically increase over time, what factor would have the greatest and most sustainable impact on your educational engine?"

Mr. Focus responded without hesitation to our question ask about factors that were critical to driving the educational engine of his school. He named two related factors—increasing the time teachers spend teaching reading skills, and providing more time for students to read during the school day.

Mr. F: I've always believed that teaching reading and ensuring kids read a lot is the most important thing elementary schools do. The kids who read the most read the best. We inherited a lot of poor readers. In fact, we started with a school where half of the kids fell below the 20th percentile in reading. Within a few years, we had very few of these kids scoring below the 20th percentile.

It was clear that Mr. Focus knew what his school was best at and that all decisions were focused on accelerating those efforts.

Q: How did you and your staff do this?

Mr. F: We emphasized reading in all of the content areas—even in math. If a program or activity was brought to our attention that wasn't about reading, we didn't do it. For instance, we use technology only for reading and math remediation. There are loads of very interesting software programs out there. Some schools are getting into using technology for product production: we didn't do that.

Instead, his staff spent more time in the school day teaching reading and giving students an opportunity to read on their own. They encouraged accelerating the bright students in addition to helping students who were at risk.

Q: Was there a particular program or process that you put into place that accelerated student performance?

Mr. F: No, unless you count our Title I program.

He explained that the teachers were really skilled and determined to do what they needed to in order to get students to read well. Given that, it did not make sense to them to hire less-skilled personnel to give poor readers a double dose of reading instruction. They knew talented trained people should be doing that work. When the staff came together to write the school-wide Title I plan and allocate funds, they agreed with Mr. Focus and decided to spend most of the funds on hiring credentialed teachers instead of instructional aides.

Mr. F: I think all of these things, along with a very creative staff working together in grade-level teams, made a big difference. We have a lot of good teachers willing to do whatever it takes to make sure kids are successful.

Mr. Focus has always felt it is his job to take the pressure off the teachers about district and state testing. In doing this, he stayed focused on the goal of students reading well.

Q: How did your school manage the pressures of district, state, and federal accountability while making these long-term changes for the future?

Mr. F: I think when students read well the test results take care of themselves. Our school's test results support my thinking that teaching reading and ensuring that kids read is the most important task elementary schools have. I don't make a big deal out of the test itself. I just emphasize things that are important for student performance—like analyzing test results for our program improvement plan every year.

Like all of the highly successful principals, Mr. Focus exhibited his aptitude for building relationships through collaborative decision making at his school, while not veering from the priorities of the school. Decision making was collegial. The school administrative staff was honest with teachers about what needed to be done.

Mr. F: If the budget needed cutting, we listed expenditures and we all prioritized them; we kept the ones with the highest priority in meeting our goals, and let go of the ones that weren't. Teachers were very much a part of that process. At Pines, the priority list generated by the teachers would look the same as if I did it myself. I was open as far as my opinions go and my reasons for them so the teachers knew exactly where I was coming from.

Mr. Focus was asked to rate what confidence he had in the decisions at the time they were made, before he knew their outcome.

Mr. F: I would give it a 10. It was obvious from the beginning that I had an excellent teaching staff and I felt good about the decisions we were making. We always ran our initial decisions through our school site council, the school's parent organization, and bilingual advisory group. They supported us.

We asked Mr. Focus what he did to ensure that teachers continued to focus on improving student performance in general and teaching reading specifically. He shared his belief that his routine presence in classrooms was critical.

Mr. F: I was in the classrooms all the time. I made tons of observations, both formal and informal. Teachers generally like this because they knew they would be having conversations with me individually, in grade-level teams, and with the staff as a whole based on what I saw in the classrooms. I was in classrooms close to two hours every day.

If Mr. Focus and the staff were betting on what drives the educational engine of Pines Elementary, their pick would always be on children gaining more skill in reading. Thus, the driving force for the educational engine at Pines Elementary School was increased skill in reading by teachers spending more time in the day teaching reading, and increased opportunities for students to read on their own.

Be Passionate About It

Mr. Focus was a fanatic when it came to the importance he placed on increasing students' reading ability. This obsession is a result of a very personal experience he had as an elementary school student.

Mr. F: One thing certainly shaped my philosophy about student learning: I didn't learn to read myself until I was in fifth grade, and so I realize the power one teacher can have on a student. My fifth-grade teacher taught me to read. I often shared that personal story with students who were struggling and with teachers who were struggling with students. I'd say, "It's not too late. Here's an opportunity to turn a student around."

His experience helped him realize that the children who can read well do the best in school.

Mr. F: My teacher used to read things to us in a dramatic way so whatever she was reading was more interesting to us. The other thing she did was to believe in me. She told my parents that nobody had taken the time to teach me to read and that she was going to make sure she did.

This focus on reading combined with a staff willing to do whatever it took to make sure students were successful resulted in profoundly higher student achievement at Pines Elementary School. The principal and staff modeled respect and effort with the students from the beginning. As a result, students at Pines Elementary felt comfortable and safe, treated each other with respect, and worked hard. Mr. Focus maintained that the school is in a win-win position when all of the necessary ingredients come together.

Ms. F: Teaching reading and ensuring that kids read is the most important thing elementary schools do. The kids who read most read
best. All of those things come together because of a staff that is
good at creatively coming up with ways to help kids read.

Thus, Mr. Focus meets the three tests of the hedgehog concept. He knows what his school can be best at—the self-motivated, self-disciplined, and talented teachers of Pines Elementary are most successful teaching students to read. Second, he knows what drives his school's educational engine—when teachers spend more time teaching reading skills and when students spend more time reading, they excel in all academic subject areas and are successful on standardized tests. Finally, he is deeply passionate about the importance of teaching reading and ensuring that students have plenty of time to read. These three tests come together to form the "one crystalline concept"(Collins, 2001, p. 95) of improving reading skills by which Mr. Focus and his staff abide in making all program and budget decisions at his school.

Recently, Mr. Focus moved back to the district office as administrator for special programs and then as an assistant superintendent for human resources. Even though he is no longer at Pines Elementary, he is content in knowing the school will keep moving forward in its quest to increase student achievement because of the strong foundation he and his teachers built during his tenure as principal. He is proud that he and the staff created a school where students are happy, parents are pleased and supportive, and students are learning.

HIGHLY SUCCESSFUL PRINCIPALS AND THE HEDGEHOG CONCEPT

All of the highly successful principals clearly demonstrate the discipline they have for staying within the three circles of the hedgehog concept. The third element of the hedgehog concept—knowing what you are deeply passionate about—was especially apparent in the responses of all the highly successful principals. The passion for Mr. Unpretentious is for building a leadership team. He had every staff member trained in that endeavor. Earlier we discussed the passion of Mr. Bond for his ability to build relationships. He believes relationships are keys to success at his school in providing a successful environment for teaching and learning. He stated, "We are on the right road because when we are dealing with curriculum and programs, the most important theme running through all this is relationships." Ms. Persevere is passionate about guided reading being conducted five days a week in every classroom, thus ensuring increased reading skills. During the first two years of her principalship, all of her efforts were calculated to achieve that goal. Ms. Discipline is passionate about creating a school environment where teachers are confident in their own abilities to successfully teach the California Standards and students show their mastery of what they have been taught. She conveys through her actions her belief that all teachers at the school are highly qualified to make professional decisions to increase student learning. She said, "Others may think you are setting targets that are too high or unrealistic. I think success comes when teachers believe they can make a difference and make the effort to meet high expectations." Finally, Ms. Aspiration's passion is in building a collaborative staff through implementing cognitive guided instruction. She maintained that "it is all about how to teach math to kids. We have a central goal and all of the staff is focused on that goal."

COMPARISON PRINCIPALS AND THE HEDGEHOG CONCEPT

Comparison principals were, as in the case of all the highly successful principals, able to describe a passion they had for their school. Ms. Ineffectual, principal of Sunkist Elementary School, is passionate about her desire for teachers at her school to take responsibility for working with the whole child and knowing that their job is to work with students when they are at school, not when they are at home. She stated, "I try to instill the philosophy that we are a village. If we miss one child, we miss them all." Ms. Conspiracy of Observatory Elementary School avowed that she is passionate about implementing a program of direct instruction at the school and would continue to concentrate her efforts on getting the staff to accept the program if it weren't for the campaign against her led by two teachers on her staff who were representatives of the teachers' association.

Whereas comparison principals could identify their passions for their schools, none of the comparison principals demonstrated through our interviews the discipline needed to stay true to their passion. The comparison principals engaged in what Collins (2001) labeled "doom loops." When these principals came to the school, they came with a new vision, a new program, and the school would lurch in that direction. Then a new vision would be seized upon, and the school would lurch in another direction. The highly successful principals were better at staying within the three circles of the hedgehog concept, allowing the momentum to build in small increments and results to be sustained—ultimately prompting a breakthrough to entirely new levels of student performance.

REFLECTION

What is the educational engine of your school or a school you know of? How does this educational engine work to increase student achievement? What does the principal do to ensure that the educational engine is focused on moving the school's vision forward?

SUGGESTIONS FOR PRINCIPALS

Knowing What You Are Best At

- Know what teachers are best at (e.g., skill and determination) and support them.
- Continually strive for excellence in the one thing that distinguishes the school as great.

Knowing What Drives Your Educational Engine

- Determine what drives the educational engine of the school (e.g., increase time spent teaching reading or increase time for students to read, or both).
- Reject programs and processes that detract the school and its teachers from driving the educational engine.

Being Passionate About It

- Live your passion every day.
- Be a fanatic about your school's educational engine.

10

Build a Culture of Discipline

If you create an environment where the people truly participate, you don't need control. They know what needs to be done, and they do it. And the more that people will devote themselves to your cause on a voluntary basis, a willing basis, the fewer hierarchs and control mechanisms you need. We are not looking for blind obedience. We're looking for people who on their own initiative want to be doing what they're doing because they consider it to be a worthy objective.

—Kelleher (1997, under "Culture Defines Personality")

THE CONCEPT IS NOT NEW

Most will agree that the idea of a "culture of discipline" is not new. The leadership literature is rich with support for the presence of an organizational culture that includes disciplined people and disciplined actions. In Chapter 12, we discuss Peters and Waterman's *In Search of Excellence* ([1982] 2004). This classic names basic principles that successful companies use. Taken together, these principles resemble the leadership behavior and characteristics described by Collins. For example, one of these principles, directly related to the concept of disciplined people who have freedom and responsibility within a framework, is "simultaneous loose-tight properties." Peters and Waterman found that excellent companies are "on one hand rigidly controlled, yet at the same time allow (indeed, insist on) autonomy, entrepreneurship, and innovation from the rank and file" (p. 318).

Peters and Waterman's work ([1982] 2004) was influenced by the work of W. Edwards Deming. Deming (as cited in DuFour, Eaker, & DuFour, 2005) found that self-managing teams generated better results with less supervision than top-down leadership (p. 146). This fits with what Collins (2001) referred to as "rinsing your cottage cheese" (p. 127), where disciplined people in the *Good to Great* companies do everything possible to fulfill their responsibilities, making excessive control unnecessary. Collins went on to emphasize that point: "When you put these two complementary forces together—a culture of discipline with an ethic of entrepreneurship—you get a magical alchemy of superior performance and sustained results" (pp. 121–122).

Mike Schmoker (2005) supported Collins' (2001) statement when he described the self-managing team.

Talent and sustained commitment are most apt to flourish in team settings that

1. combine autonomy *and* responsibility for results, and

2. provide abundant opportunities for individuals to share their collective and complementary skills and abilities toward better results. (Schmoker, p. 146)

Another example of the Peters and Waterman ([1982] 2004) principles follows the same line of thinking as the hedgehog concept's concept of knowing what the organization does the best and focusing all efforts in that area. Their principle of "sticking to the knitting" centers on remaining with the business the company knows best. Peters and Waterman found that companies that stick to their knitting were more successful than companies that diversified.

DIFFICULTIES IN ACHIEVING
A CULTURE OF DISCIPLINE

A culture of discipline encompasses all the attributes that we have examined thus far in this book. In Chapter 7, we examined the highly successful principals for their ability to get the right teachers (disciplined people) for their school. The personal humility, compelling modesty, and ambition for their school's success displayed by the principals we studied in Chapters 3, 4, and 5 serve as a signal to others that everyone in the organization is valued for his or her own disciplined contributions. In Chapters 3 and 6, we saw the disciplined thought of all these principals manifested in their unwavering resolve and professional will in confronting the brutal facts of reality while being persistent in believing that they would be successful in dealing with that reality. Chapters 2 and 9 demonstrated that these principals were able to successfully build relationships with all members of their school community to fine-tune the discipline of their actions in adhering to their hedgehog concept.

With the exception of Mr. Focus—the principal who opened a new school and hired all of the teachers at that time—all of the highly successful principals we studied built a culture of discipline at a school where it was not in place before their arrival. To guide us in unearthing evidence for building a culture of discipline in their interview responses, we drew on Collins' (2001) amplification on the subject:

1. Build a culture around the ideas of freedom and responsibility, within a framework.

2. Fill that culture with self-disciplined people who are willing to go to extreme lengths to fulfill their responsibilities.

3. Don't confuse a culture of discipline with a tyrannical disciplinarian.

4. Adhere with great consistency to the Hedgehog Concept, exercising an almost religious focus on the intersection of the three circles. Equally important, create a "stop doing list" and systematically unplug anything extraneous. (p. 124)

On the one hand, a highly successful principal gives teachers the freedom to determine the best path for achieving their objectives (that is, he or she protects teachers from district, state, and federal mandates, and does not manage them). On the other hand, these principals say "No" to teacher proposals that fail the three circles test of the hedgehog concept. All of these highly successful principals maintain a vision of improving student achievement. They are able to gather together disciplined people who are engaged in disciplined thought and who then take disciplined action to support the principal's vision.

Using these four elements as our lens, we turn now to understand the culture of discipline built by all of the highly successful principals in our study. First, we explore the case of Ms. Discipline of Eagle Elementary School.

MS. DISCIPLINE AND
EAGLE ELEMENTARY SCHOOL

Eagle Elementary School is in a suburban neighborhood school nestled in the center of an upwardly mobile community in California. Approximately 69% of the students are white, 16% are Hispanic, and 6% are African American. The principal characterizes the parents of the school's students as "caring and involved." Many of the households consist of single-wage earners and stay-at-home mothers. The school benefits by having a lot of parent volunteers. The student to teacher ratio is 20 to 1. The school is a high performer on the mandated California State Testing, sustaining a statewide Academic Performance Index (API) decile relative ranking of 9 or 10 during the five-year period between 1999 and 2004, and earning a California Distinguished Schools Award. More noteworthy is the school's trend toward improvement when compared to schools in other upwardly mobile communities like theirs. Table 10.1 shows impressive improvement beginning with a rank of decile 6 and moving to a rank of 9 or 10 in the following years.

Table 10.1   Eagle Elementary School: API Relative Rank and Similar Schools Rank

	1999	2000	2001	2002	2003	2004
Relative Rank	9	9	10	10	10	10
Similar Schools Rank	6	6	9	10	9	10

The mission of the school is articulated as follows: "In a cooperative effort, staff, students, and community are committed to building a strong foundation for the advancement of learning, providing a motivating and positive environment to meet the diverse needs and abilities of the students."

The beauty of Eagle Elementary School impressed us immediately as we walked through its front doors. An ambience of openness in the actual physical layout of the school welcomed us. We walked through the front office area to the top of gentle stairs that led down to a place where the library filled an open space in the center of the school. Open doors to the classrooms lined the perimeter of the open space.

The principal's office, just to the right of the front office area, had floor-to-ceiling sliding glass doors that took up two of the office walls and allowed a full view of the library and several classrooms. Ms. Discipline was sitting at her desk facing those wonderful glass doors when we walked into her office. We introduced ourselves, sat down so that we, too, could look out the glass doors, and asked our first question:

Q: What do you think of your office?

Ms. D: Believe it or not, I'm hardly ever in my office. I expected you, so here I am. I *can* say there is very little need to decorate the walls— I already have a beautiful view through these windows!

Surround Yourself With Self-Disciplined People

We were eager to get to the heart of what was happening at this school to result in so much success. Ms. Discipline's response to the next question was evidence that she came to a school where a culture of discipline was not firmly established. A culture of discipline began to take shape as she hired disciplined, self-confident, and talented people who were focused and motivated to do what was necessary to promote student learning.

Ms. D: Over the years, we had multitrack and our staff [is] very large. Then we moved back to a traditional schedule and we lost folks. With all of those changes, each time I was able to add more excellent teachers who share my passions here and keep them. I believe there are only five folks who were leftovers that have been here all along.

Besides being able to get the right people over the years, she also demonstrated her ability to eliminate staff that was were not a fit with the culture of discipline of Eagle Elementary School.

Ms. D: When I first got here, the staff was fragmented. The previous principal apparently had been playing one grade level against another. I observed one grade-level team copying their reading books on the Xerox because they could not get the materials, while another grade level had multiple resources for a given content area. There were definite inequities among the grade levels. In addition, some folks in the first-grade level were very close to the previous principal and really didn't make life pleasant for anybody. They were argumentative and outspoken about things they wanted.

She described her reaction to these difficult staff members.

Ms. D: I made a conscious decision that I would not allow them to change the way I behaved, so I didn't [change my behavior] and they transferred—not that year, but the next year.

Ms. Discipline talked about the fierce competitive spirit of the staff.

Ms. D: There is intense competitiveness on the part of the staff, not between themselves, but with other schools. It really ticks them off that other schools might beat us [in test scores].

Ms. Discipline described her leadership style as a consensus builder. It is interesting to us that she should describe herself in that way, because she gave us plenty of evidence that coming to consensus was not necessary with her staff.

Q: How did you get commitment and agreement with decisions from everyone?

Ms. D: It never occurred to me that they wouldn't follow along.

She has definite beliefs and high expectations for her staff and students and she makes certain that they know what those are. We already know that she will assist any staff members to transfer if they do not share those beliefs and expectations. Given the disciplined people on her staff, and given that their beliefs are in alignment with those of Ms. Discipline, what is there to come to agreement about?

Build a Culture Around the
Ideas of Freedom and Responsibility

When a school has disciplined people, the principal has less need for excessive control, freeing teachers to be more productive and innovative. Ms. Discipline described with clarity a responsible teaching staff that did not need managing. Her task was to manage the school as a system instead.

Ms. D: These teachers are highly educated and disciplined people who spend a lot of time figuring out what their students need without me having to tell them they need to do that. They certainly do not need managing. My job is to honor that and [to] support them in any way I can.

Q: In what ways do you support them?

Ms. D: I get them the materials and staff development they need and ask for. I deal with parent issues when I can. I see that the buses arrive and leave on time. You know, things like that. Sometimes I feel that they want so much to do things to please me that I find myself convincing them that it is a good thing to take risks and try something different. I want people to be the best they can be. The only way they can do that is by trying new things.

Q: What kind of leadership style would your teachers say you have?

Ms. D: They know I'm a good listener and trust them to do what they need to do to teach their students.

Q: Can you give me an example of a situation where this happened?

Ms. D: The district adopted new books. I told the teachers to do what works [for teaching the California essential content standards] and use the district materials as a resource; but please, don't throw the baby [the effective things they do] out with the bath water.

Ms. Discipline shared an event that had occurred the year before to demonstrate how her teachers took a stand to fulfill their responsibilities for increasing student learning.

Ms. D: Last year, salary and benefits were being negotiated between the teachers' association and the district. The teachers' association was stirring the pot across the district. However, at our school, it was business as usual. Our teachers made no fuss. There were no picketing signs in the front of the school and our association representatives for the school only did what they were required to do.

Don't Confuse a Culture of Discipline With Tyranny

The interview with Ms. Discipline offered no evidence that Eagle Elementary School's leader is a tyrannical disciplinarian or that the school is ruled by rules and regulations. When Ms. Discipline was asked to share something that exemplifies the essence of the success of her school, she described a certain "feeling tone."

Ms. D: You feel the way the school works when you walk in the front door. The front office staff makes people feel wonderful, warm, and welcome. Substitute teachers have commented about that. The staff and student teachers have all made mention of how helpful people are here. There is support everywhere you look. You know that people care. The whole staff gathers [people in need] up. That's what we do. We are family here. Teachers are serious about what they are doing every minute with kids.

Once again, a highly successful principal related important purposes for visiting classrooms often that, in this case, were examples of her promotion of a culture of discipline through a sense of shared professional growth.

Ms. D: I'm in classrooms every day. When I observe formally or informally in a classroom, I always follow up with individual teachers and together we talk about next steps—what the teacher will do and how I will offer support. I schmooze the staff. I know that one of the things that is so fascinating about this is there is always room for all of us to do something different and better. Sometimes, when I'm doing a formal observation and I see the lesson is bombing, I tell the teacher I'll come back another day. I'm not there to say, Gotcha! I would rather see what is really happening on a day-to-day basis than watch a dog and pony show that isn't working.

Adhere With Great Consistency to the Hedgehog Concept

A culture of discipline in a school involves constantly striving for excellence in the one thing that distinguishes it as a great school and rejecting programs and processes that might detract the school and its teachers from being best. Ms. Discipline exhibited her understanding of the importance of simplicity and eliminating anything that does not promote improving student performance. We heard evidence for this understanding when she shared that she did not require teachers to use only the materials newly adopted by the district when the materials they were using were working. Another example of adhering to the hedgehog concept was heard when she stated, "We promote the idea of not wasting kids' time by preassessing to find out what they know and teaching what they don't know."

Know What They Are Best At

Ms. Discipline knows her teachers are highly qualified to make professional decisions and affords them the leeway to make professional decisions about instruction, with or without approval from the district office. We shared evidence of this earlier in the section in this chapter on building a culture around the ideas of freedom and responsibility.

Know What Drives the Educational Engine

Ms. Discipline knows what drives the educational engine at Eagle Elementary School.

Ms. D: We are guaranteed that student performance will improve because we all focus on teaching the California Content Standards. I also believe success comes when teachers believe they can make a difference and make the effort to meet high expectations.

Be Passionate About It

She lives her passion every day by creating a school environment where teachers are confident in their own abilities to successfully teach the California Standards, and where students show their mastery of what they have been taught. She is passionate about the support she gives her teachers and her high expectations for teachers teaching and students learning.

When Ms. Discipline leaves Eagle Elementary, she would like to have people remember that she has extremely high expectations, that she supports her staff's hard work, and that she appreciates their willingness to take risks. She demonstrates the enjoyment she gains from her role as principal at the school when she says, "It would be fun to see if I could replicate the joy here [at Eagle Elementary School] at a new school."

HIGHLY SUCCESSFUL PRINCIPALS AND A CULTURE OF DISCIPLINE

A few more examples of highly successful principals exhibiting a culture of discipline here serve to solidify our findings. Mr. Focus described his staff as self-disciplined and self-motivated to implement a program focusing on teaching reading. His philosophy was shared by the teachers who worked diligently to provide an environment where students are successful. The staff is positive, collegial, and noncompetitive with each other. They are free to take on challenges to find a solution and are willing to put in the time to deal with it. Mr. Unpretentious' staff is trained in shared leadership and makes most decisions as a team. Every member of the staff at Mr. Bond's school plays an active role in a collaborative team, thanks to years of focus on building relationships.

COMPARISON PRINCIPALS AND A CULTURE OF DISCIPLINE

What is missing with the comparison principal responses is discussion about the self-discipline and self-motivation of the staff. Ms. Ineffectual of Sunkist Elementary School expresses hope, but not certainty, that her staff is self-motivated enough to continue when she is no longer principal of the school. She said, "I think I'd be most proud that I can leave the school with teachers that are knowledgeable and want to be here and want to continue the work we have started." On the other hand, Ms. Relinquish of Johnson Elementary said, "I'm a hands-off leader and expect the teachers to do their jobs professionally, but if a teacher is not performing, I do step up to the plate." One wonders if the freedom she gives her teachers is not because she trusts them to be professional, but because the union power at the school intimidates her.

Each of the comparison principals relates experiences that suggest they are in various stages of developing a culture of discipline, where everyone adheres to a consistent system and where teachers are given freedom and responsibilities. All of the highly successful principals understand the importance of building a culture of discipline and are all successful in promoting such a culture at their schools.

REFLECTION

When thinking about building the culture of a school, what criteria should be considered when selecting the actions or activities to be used to ensure that a culture of discipline is established that leads to increased student performance?

SUGGESTIONS FOR PRINCIPALS

Building a Culture Around the Ideas of Freedom and Responsibility

- Establish goals and a vision, and stay firm but not tyrannical about them.
- Encourage staff input and innovation.
- Emphasize collaboration.
- Encourage teacher freedom and responsibility within the agreed on goals and vision.

Filling the Culture With Self-Disciplined People

- Establish clear expectations.
- Hire staff who are disciplined, self-confident, focused, productive, and motivated to do what is necessary to promote student learning.
- Provide support for staff with materials, personnel, and staff development.

Adhering Consistently to the Hedgehog Concept

- Adhere to the three circles rule: Know what your school and staff is best at. Know what drives the educational engine of the school. Be passionate about it.

11

Know Commonalities and Differences Between Public Schools and the Private Sector

Our Similarities bring us to a common ground; Our Differences allow us to be fascinated by each other.

—Tom Robbins, author (1936–)

A reminder to the reader may be useful at this point. The research by Collins (2001) in his book *Good to Great* has been used here to consider school principals. We found many interesting overlaps between the Collins study and our study of principals. At the same time, there are parts that don't fit precisely, as was the case when we examined getting the right people on the bus, or when we endeavored to define what drives the educational engine in our application of the hedgehog concept to school leadership. We know there are important differences between school organizations and the private sector, just as we know that certain leadership attributes are relevant for both the private sector and schools. We will discuss some of the differences first.

DISPARITIES BETWEEN PUBLIC SCHOOLS AND THE PRIVATE SECTOR

We view the following differences as critical to any study comparing schools with the private sector: (1) A student is not a product. (2) Schools and the private sector have different purposes. (3) There is a distinction between the authority of principals and the authority of CEOs. (4) Schools have an approach to determining success that is different from the private sector's approach.

A Student Is Not a Product

Paula Dawning, former executive at AT&T and currently superintendent of Benton Harbor Area Schools, Benton Harbor, Michigan, related what she learned as a new superintendent: "When I lost a big account in the business world, it would bother me. But it wasn't like I was messing with someone's life. Education is different. We're talking about preparing children for their lives. If we mess up, that child is not going to get that chance back" (LaFee, 2004, under "Peer Influence").

Cuban (2006), in a recent article titled "Why Can't Schools Be Like Businesses," retold a story that a successful executive had shared with him. Jamie Volmer was an executive at a successful ice cream company whose blueberry-flavored ice cream had the honor of being named "Best Blueberry Ice Cream in America" by *People* magazine. He was giving a presentation to a group of educators about the importance of looking to business to make changes needed in schools and was promoting the business community's knack for producing quality. Here is what transpired following his presentation:

> A woman's hand shot up. She began quietly, "We are told, sir, that you manage a company that makes good ice cream." I smugly

replied, "Best ice cream in America, ma'am." "How nice," she said. "Is it rich and smooth?" "Sixteen percent butterfat," I crowed. . . . I never saw the next line coming. "Mr. Vollmer," she said, learning forward with a wicked eyebrow raised to the sky, "When you are standing on your receiving dock and you see an inferior shipment of blueberries arrive, what do you do?" In the silence of that room, I could hear the trap snap. I was dead meat, but I wasn't going to lie. "I send them back." "That's right," she barked, "and we can never send back our blueberries. We take them big, small, rich, poor, gifted, exceptional, abused, frightened, confident, homeless, rude . . . we take them all. Everyone. That, Mr. Vollmer, is why it's not a business. It's a school." (pp. 1–2)

Different Purposes

School districts perform functions similar to those of business organizations—managing people, planning, budgeting, and so on. However, the expectations are that school districts meet public and political responsibilities for their actions and student outcomes. This accountability is absent from for-profit institutions.

Whereas for-profit organizations also have multiple purposes, these purposes are usually for increasing total revenues, net profits, and dividends to investors. Private sector companies seldom mention shaping literacy and civic duty as their purposes. The reason is simple enough—school districts are public endeavors meant to enhance the collective interests, not individual interests.

Thomas Sergiovanni (1996) was in agreement with this difference between school organizations and business organizations. Sergiovanni warned that applying business success models to education is inappropriate given the unique nature of schools. Specifically, Sergiovanni argued that "good leadership for corporations and other organizations . . . may not be good leadership for . . . social enterprises. . . . Everything that happens in the schoolhouse has moral overtones that are virtually unmatched by other institutions in our society" (p. xii). In other words, schooling is intrinsically value-laden because it shapes the lives of students and, thus, our culture and society.

Distinctions in Authority

In the private sector, corporate leaders are often selected by boards of directors who make decisions behind closed doors without the public or journalists in attendance. On the other hand, elected school boards are obliged by law to consider, debate, and make decisions in public. Of equal importance, school board decisions are subject to media and public scrutiny. Not so in for-profit organizations.

Throughout the chapters in this book, we have discussed the very real disparity between the authority of chief executive officers of corporations with that of school leaders. Collins (2005) hypothesized that there are two types of leadership skill: executive and legislative. Legislative authority relies more on persuasion, political currency, and shared interests (p. 11). He gave us an example from the social sector when he cited Frances Hesselbein, Girl Scout CEO. She stated,

> Oh, you always have power, if you just know where to find it. There is the power of inclusion, and the power of language, and the power of shared interests, and the power of coalition. Power is all around you to draw upon, but it is rarely raw, rarely visible. (p. 10)

We position school principal authority in the legislative corner and CEO authority in the executive corner. In our study, we observed a strong element of persuasiveness—sometimes in the form of schmoozing, as in the cases of Ms. Persevere and Ms. Discipline—among the highly successful principals. Even when the authority of school leaders is restricted due to federal, state, and district policy; procedures; and contract language, the highly successful principals in our study were able to succeed in leading their schools to greatness.

Contrary Approaches for Determining Success

There is a difference in how success is perceived, of course. In business, profits are the economic engine. It is all about making money. In education, it is not as clear because we are talking about educating children, not selling a product. Even so, you can tell when something is or is not working. You can figure out what the educational engine is and what drives it. With the multiple purposes that schools are expected to achieve and the variety of customers the schools are expected to serve, one would expect multiple criteria for determining whether schools are successful. However, quite the opposite has occurred. Over the past 30 years, tests to measure achievement in a few academic areas, along with rewards and penalties for performance, have been the norm. This focus on test scores as a single measure of success has been a dubiously successful attempt to copy the bottom line of profit-making companies—which is a narrow gauge of success.

Sergiovanni's (1996) arguments were convincing. We agree that it would be a mistake to directly apply every insight gained from fields outside education to school leadership issues. Nonetheless, we believe it is helpful to consider business leadership successes, given the question we began with in Chapter 1: "We know what to do, so why do we fail?" In this book, however, we accomplish our examination of the characteristics and behaviors of a select group of effective school principals through a school leadership lens.

WHAT WE HAVE LEARNED FROM THE RESEARCH ON LEADERSHIP

Even with the disparities between school leadership and business leadership described earlier, many leadership attributes are recognized as relevant for schools as well as the private sector. In fact, we believe the numerous attributes shared by both school and private sector leadership far outweigh the differences. We examined Collins' (2001) research pertaining to his Level 5 Executive as we moved through previous chapters in this book, and the evidence for leadership qualities relevant to both schools and the private sector was apparent. Every one of the principals in our study—highly successful and comparison principals alike—shared occasions when three additional behaviors were met with a degree of success or failure. These behaviors are

1. displaying and building trust,

2. promoting participative governance and professional learning communities, and

3. management by wandering around.

These three behaviors have influenced the work of school and business leaders alike and are, as evidenced in our interviews with school principals, applicable to our study.

Displaying and Building Trust

We like people who are trustworthy and seek them out as friends. We listen to people we trust and accept their influence. Thus, the most effective leadership situations are those in which members of the team trust one another. We discuss trust here because we believe it is a necessary underlying element needed in order for any of the leadership characteristics and behaviors identified in the Collins (2001) study as well as our separate finding of building relationships to be effective.

Several major research studies support the influence of trust in exemplary private sector leaders (Bennis, 1984; Brunard & Kleiner, 1994; Kouzes & Posner, 2002). The importance of trust to organizational success was highlighted as early as 1972 in a study conducted by Dale Zand, a professor at New York University, in which he looked at trust and managerial problem solving effectiveness. He reported the following:

> Apparently in low trust groups, interpersonal relationships interfere with and distort perceptions of the problem. Energy and creativity are diverted from finding comprehensive, realistic solutions, and

members use the problem as an instrument to minimize their vulnerability. In contrast, in high trust groups, there is less socially generated uncertainty and problems are solved more effectively. (Asherman, Bing, & Laroche, 2000, under "The Importance of Trust")

When considering leader trust, Taylor McConnell, author of *Group Leadership for Self Realization,* stated,

The most productive people are the most trusting people. If this seems to be an astonishing statement, it shows how distorted the concept of trust has become. Trust is one of the most essential qualities of human relationships. Without it, all human interaction, all commerce, all society would disappear. (Asherman, Bing, & Laroche, 2000, under "The Importance of Trust")

On the educational side of the house, Blase and Kirby (2000) found that the most influential features of principals' personalities are their honesty, optimism, and consideration, all of which lead to building a trusting relationship with others. From trust, teachers reported a promotion of collaboration, teacher satisfaction, and effort. Other school leadership studies on trust established that the school principal is the key person in developing trust, both by demonstrating it and by fostering a culture of trusted relationships in the school (Bryk & Schneider, 2002; Fullan, 2003).

Highly Successful Principals and Displaying and Building Trust

Our interviews with highly successful principals yielded evidence for displaying and building trust. Mr. Unpretentious developed leadership among his teachers and, in doing so, displayed his trust in their abilities. Teachers, in turn trusted him.

Mr. U: What I try to do is involve people. I don't think of myself as the leader. I think of myself as just one of the leaders at this school. I can't remember a time when I made a decision on my own. In fact, there were times when the teachers presented their own decision and I agreed. I think teachers felt empowered when this happened. They certainly weren't afraid to approach me with any idea they had.

Participative Governance and Professional Learning Communities

We looked at two areas within the field of shared decision making: participative governance and professional learning communities.

Participative Governance

All of the principals in our study described processes of collaboration. Besides our earlier reference to W. Edwards Deming's self-managing teams and Mike Schmoker's support for the process, other scholars have conducted research on this topic. Participative management, focusing on human motivation and its impact on job satisfaction and productivity, was the focus of several landmark studies (Blake & McCanse, 1991; Drucker, 1954; Hertzberg, 1959; Likert, 1967; Maslow, 1943). Blake and McCanse developed their "leadership grid." The most desirable type of leadership in this grid was one in which there is team management, work is accomplished by committed people, and there is interdependence through a common stake in organizational purpose. In a more recent study, Kim (2002) stated, "Participation is a process in which influence is shared among individuals who are otherwise hierarchical unequals" (p. 232). Kim's study was based on information collected from the Clark County, Nevada, employee survey conducted in 1999 that involved 1,576 employees. The results of the study show that leaders' uses of a participative management style are positively associated with high levels of job satisfaction, especially when effective communications are an integral component of the process.

In a study of the school reform process, Coch and French (1948) found that employees who were given the opportunity to play a role in goal setting and making decisions that affect their work accepted change more readily. Covey (1989) reasoned that trust is the amount of safeness we feel with others. In an atmosphere of trust, teachers and principals are able to work together to identify and solve problems. Shared governance principles foster this kind of environment in schools. Blase and Blase (1994) established through their research that an effective principal exhibits behaviors that support shared governance when he or she (1) encourages openness, (2) facilitates effective communication, and (3) models understanding. Effective principals encourage teacher involvement, eliminate issues of risk and threat, and facilitate empowerment. Peters and Waterman ([1982] 2004) posited that the hallmark of any successful organization is a shared sense among its members about what they are trying to accomplish.

Allen, Glickman, and Hensley (1998) found evidence of improved student achievement, lower dropout rates, gains in teachers' critical thinking skills, and improved school climate in Georgia schools that gave teachers a voice in school governance.

Professional Learning Communities

More recently, "professional learning communities" has emerged as a refinement of earlier ideas about participative management and shared decision making. It is discussed here because districts across California and the rest of the nation currently are reading about and implementing professional learning communities. At the time of our interviews, not one of the principals we spoke with used the term "professional learning community" when describing his or her decision-making processes. Instead, terms such as "collaboration" and "teamwork" were the words of choice. Today, the important differences between professional learning communities and other collaborative efforts are of interest to us, given our understanding of the importance of having a culture of discipline, the hedgehog concept, and building relationships, and all that they entail. From Richard DuFour (2005), we learn that professional learning communities take the concept of collaboration, grade-level teams, and departments to a higher level. There is no better way to state what DuFour believes is the biggest shift in thinking when making collaborative efforts in a professional learning community than when he described it as a "simple shift—from a focus on teaching to a focus on learning" (p. 32). The work that people within a professional learning community engage in is structured around the exploration of three important questions:

- How do we want each student to learn?
- How will we know when each student has learned it?
- How will we respond when a student experiences difficulty in learning? (p. 33)

Highly Successful Principals and Professional Learning Communities

We have evidence from our interviews with highly successful principals that these three questions were the basis for their disciplined efforts in working collaboratively with their teachers. We noted that their descriptions of collaborative work in most chapters of this book resembled professional learning communities: they just didn't use the label during our interviews. Our conversation with Ms. Discipline is a good example. She addressed the question of how we want children to learn as follows:

Ms. D: Let me give you an example of the process we use for all of our instructional decisions here. At the beginning of this year during our staff development days, we got together and brainstormed successful best practices for teaching the California Standards. We all agreed that we would implement certain of the practices that we discussed. I told the teachers that I would be looking specifically for those practices when I visit classrooms.

She talked about how she and her staff know students have learned with this response:

Ms. D: Then, late in the year, we came together as a team to look at the results of the CST [the California Standards Test].

Finally, she explained how they respond when a student experiences difficulty in learning, as follows:

Ms. D: The exciting part came when we collaborated on plans for helping kids who didn't do well on the test. Again, I told the teachers I would be visiting classrooms and looking for evidence that we were following through with our plans.

Management by Wandering Around

In every one of the interviews we conducted in our research, principals cited "being in classrooms often" as a priority in their work. This notion of leaders being out and about has its roots in business organizational literature, as well as in educational literature. Management by wandering around is the informal supervision of general management; it is a practice commonly found in business. One of the eight attributes that emerged to characterize the excellent companies in the Peters and Waterman ([1982] 2004) research was what they termed "hands-on, value driven" (p.15). CEOs of companies where this attribute prevailed were often found walking their plant floors and visiting their stores. Larry Frase (1998; Frase, Zhu, & Galloway, 2001) found that frequency of principal classroom visits predicted teacher perceived efficacy of others and teacher perceptions of organizational effectiveness. Chester and Beaudin (1996) studied the effects of principal presence in classrooms of newly hired teachers in urban schools and reported that teachers whose principals frequently visited their classrooms exhibited higher teacher self-efficacy, higher perceived efficacy of other teachers, and higher perceived efficacy of the school. In more recent studies (Frase, 2003; Freedman & Lafleur, 2002), further evidence was found demonstrating that frequency of principal classroom visits has a powerful impact on teacher perceived efficacy, teacher perceived organizational effectiveness, teacher value of teacher appraisal and professional development, and frequency of teacher flow experiences.

A number of studies (Andrews & Soder, 1987; Freedman & Lafleur, 2002; Heck, Larsen, & Marcoulides, 1990; Sagor, 1992) offer evidence that when the principals are in classrooms frequently, working on curriculum and instructional problems, and making curriculum and instruction their Number One priority, there is an improved teacher perception of principal effectiveness.

For many years, teachers and parents have identified student discipline and student lack of respect for teachers as the biggest roadblocks to improved educational practices and improved student achievement. Studies in the 1980s (Blase, 1985; Blase & Blase, 1986; Greenfield & Blase, 1981) found that principal visibility in classrooms and placing curriculum and instruction at the top of school priorities are strongly linked to improved student discipline and acceptance of advice and criticism from teachers and principals. Studies by Andrews, Soder, and Jacoby (1986) and Hallinger and Heck (1996) suggest that the benefit is greater for low-income and low-achieving students.

Highly Successful Principals and Management by Wandering Around

All of the principals in our study—both highly successful and comparison—mentioned classroom visits as an important way of ensuring that teachers continued to focus on improving student performance. However, this endeavor was most effective when combined with the leadership attributes of the highly successful principals we have examined in previous chapters. For example, Mr. Focus applied his knowledge of what his school's educational engine was (teachers teaching reading effectively and students reading often) when observing in classrooms.

Mr. F: I was in classrooms all the time. I made many formal and informal observations.

Q: What were you looking for when you visited classrooms?

Mr. F: I was looking for many things but mainly I was looking for how effective teachers were teaching reading skills. I also expected that when I visited a classroom, there would be times where students were reading independently.

Our purposes in this chapter have been to address the numerous discussions among academics about the difference between school leadership and private sector leadership and the qualities common to both. The discussion here in this chapter along with the information gleaned from our study of highly successful principals in past chapters is critical as we now consider implications for the reform of public school administrator preparation programs.

REFLECTION

Explain how the statement "A student is not a product" helps define the work of school leadership in the twenty-first century.

How are trust, participative governance, professional learning communities, and frequent classroom visits interdependent?

SUGGESTIONS FOR PRINCIPALS

Building Trust

- Be honest.
- Be optimistic.
- Be considerate.
- Develop leadership among staff and, in doing so, display trust in their abilities.
- Foster a culture of trusted relationships among staff, students, and parents.

Promoting Participative Governance and Professional Learning Communities

- Provide opportunities for staff to play a significant role in goal setting, problem solving, and making decisions that affect their work.
- Encourage openness in others.
- Facilitate effective communication.
- Encourage teacher involvement, eliminating issues of risk and threat.
- Shift thinking from a focus on teaching to a focus on learning.
- Use DuFour's (2005) three questions to engage conversation across the school:
  - How do we want each student to learn?
  - How will we know when each student has learned it?
  - How will we respond when a student experiences difficulty in learning? (p. 33)

Getting Into Classrooms Often

- Schedule dedicated time each day to visit classrooms.
- Focus on curriculum and instructional issues when visiting classrooms. Communicate this focus with teachers prior to visiting.
- Make it clear to teachers your purpose for visiting, whether for formal or informal observations. Is your purpose to evaluate or to provide support?

12

Support Research-Based Principal Preparation

Teaching is the only major occupation of man for which we have not yet developed tools that make an average person capable of competence and performance. In teaching we rely on the "naturals," the ones who somehow know how to teach. . . . Nobody seems to know, however, what it is the "naturals" do that the rest of us do not do.

—Drucker (1968, p. 338)

During the past twenty-five years, a sizable pile of evidence has been accumulated to support the notion that the principal plays a major role in the success of a school and the achievement of its students. It seems strange, therefore, that sound, research-based knowledge about how to prepare great principals is, at best, sparse (Davis, Darling-Hammond, LaPointe, & Meyerson, 2005).

THE ISLLC STANDARDS

Our awareness of this lack of empirical data became acute not long ago when we were charged with developing a new principal preparation program at San Diego State University (SDSU). More specifically, the Educational Leadership Department needed to adjust its program to conform to the new standards released by the California Department of Education. As it turned out, the new standards were in many respects simply a rehash of the old content. We were not surprised to learn that many of our sister universities were revising their preparation programs without making substantive content changes. Ours didn't require a single change in the course catalog.

The new standards adopted by the State of California were modifications of the standards developed previously by the Interstate School Leaders Licensure Consortium (ISLLC), a project of the Council of Chief State School Officers in collaboration with the National Policy Board for Educational Administration. It is fair to say that these standards were based on empirical research whenever possible. However, as we noted above, not much solid research exists, so the authors of the standards relied on lots of craft knowledge—which they usually passed off as best practices. As we mentioned in the preface to this book, these newly crafted standards were validated by asking practicing administrators, experts, and other stakeholders in the educational enterprise to review them (Murphy, 2005, p. 166). The result of this process was a consensus about what should be included in the preparation of school administrators. Missing was the research base connecting these standards with student performance—the ultimate mission of schools. In other words, we don't have solid evidence that all or even most of the ISLLC standards make a difference in the preparation of high-quality school administrators.

A similar process was repeated at the state level using the ISLLC standards as a model. We were invited to be representatives of the California Association of School Administrators and spend a day helping to develop California's version of the ISLLC standards. The task force assembled included congenial people with varying experience in education, including a couple of education administration professors, employee association representatives, and practicing school employees and school administrators. After an hour or so, we were convinced that few in the room were qualified either by training or by experience to participate in the establishment of quality standards for school leaders. None of the brainstorming and other conversations taking place that day centered on improving pupil achievement. Participating in the day's deliberations was both eye-opening and stultifying. Later, as we struggled with our program redesign task at SDSU, we couldn't help thinking of that day.

We are convinced the approach to research on leadership Collins (2001) used in *Good to Great* is sound. He and his associates zeroed in on the connection between institutional greatness and the characteristics and behaviors of institutional leaders. This is the missing link in many of the ISLLC standards. Our project represents one small step toward addressing the question of whether Collins' research on great private sector leadership is applicable to public schools. With the exception of the focus on profit inherent in private sector institutions, we think it is applicable.

THE MID-CONTINENT RESEARCH FOR EDUCATION AND LEARNING

Recently, another organization has stepped up to the plate to provide the critical research links. Mid-continent Research for Education and Learning (McREL) developed *McREL's Balanced Leadership Framework* (Waters, Marzano, & McNulty, 2003) in an effort to "add value to the use of the ISLLC standards for the preparation, licensure, and professional development of school leaders" (Waters & Grubb, 2004, p. 2). The framework is composed of 21 principal responsibilities and 66 corresponding leadership practices that have statistically significant relationships with student achievement. McREL's findings were based on 70 studies combined for the purpose of meta-analysis. The studies represented a sample size of 2,894 schools and approximately 14,000 teachers and 1.1 million students. If sample size means anything, this was a major study. The framework is presented in Table 12.1.

An examination of the responsibilities and associated practices identified by McREL revealed many activities that Collins (2001) clustered into his chapters describing what the great CEOs do. One can only wonder how these data might correlate with Collins' findings.

IN SEARCH OF EXCELLENCE

Collins' (2001) approach to his research was not entirely novel. For example, in 1982, Peters and Waterman's ([1982] 2004) famous book *In Search of*

(Text continued on page 120)

Table 12.1   McREL's Balanced Leadership Framework Responsibilities, Average *r*, and Associated Practices

Responsibility	Definition: The Extent to Which the Principal . . .	Average **r**	Associated Practices
Affirmation	. . . recognizes and celebrates school accomplishments and acknowledges failures.	.25	• Systematically and fairly recognizes and celebrates accomplishments of teachers and staff • Systematically and fairly recognizes and celebrates accomplishments of students • Systematically and fairly acknowledges failures and celebrates accomplishments of the school
Change Agent	. . . is willing to and actively challenges the status quo.	.30	• Consciously challenges the status quo • Is comfortable leading change initiatives with uncertain outcomes • Systematically considers new and better ways of doing things
Communication	. . . establishes strong lines of communication with teachers and among stakeholders.	.23	• Is easily accessible to teachers and staff • Develops effective means for teachers and staff to communicate with one another • Maintains open and effective lines of communication with teachers and staff
Contingent Rewards	. . . recognizes and rewards individual accomplishments.	.15	• Recognizes individuals who excel • Uses performance vs. seniority as the primary criterion for reward and advancement • Uses hard work and results as the basis for reward and recognition

(Continued)

Table 12.1 (Continued)

Responsibility	Definition: The Extent to Which the Principal . . .	Average r	Associated Practices
Culture	. . . fosters shared beliefs and a sense of community and cooperation.	.29	• Promotes cooperation among teachers and staff • Promotes a sense of well-being • Promotes cohesion among teachers and staff • Develops an understanding of purpose • Develops a shared vision of what the school could be like
Curriculum, Instruction, Assessment	. . . is directly involved in the design and implementation of curriculum, instruction, and assessment practices.	.16	• Is involved with teachers in designing curricular activation and addressing instructional issues in their classrooms • Is involved with teachers to address assessment issues
Discipline	. . . protects teachers from issues and influences that would detract from their teaching time or focus.	.24	• Protects instructional time from interruptions • Protects/shelters teachers from distractions
Flexibility	. . . adapts his or her leadership behavior to the needs of the current situation and is comfortable with dissent.	.22	• Is comfortable with major changes in how things are done • Encourages people to express opinions that may be contrary to those held by individuals in positions of authority • Adapts leadership style to needs of specific situations • Can be directive or nondirective as the situation warrants
Focus	. . . establishes clear goals and keeps those goals in the forefront of the school's attention.	.24	• Establishes high, concrete goals and the expectation that all students will meet them • Establishes high, concrete goals for all curricula, instruction, and assessment

			• Establishes high, concrete goals for the general functioning of the school • Keeps everyone's attention focused on established goals
Ideals/Beliefs	.25	. . . communicates and operates from strong ideals and beliefs about schooling.	• Holds strong professional ideals and beliefs about schooling, teaching, and learning • Shares ideals and beliefs about schooling, teaching, and learning with teachers, staff, and parents • Demonstrates behaviors that are consistent with ideals and beliefs
Input	.30	. . . involves teachers in the design and implementation of important decisions and policies.	• Provides opportunities for input from teachers and staff on all important decisions • Provides opportunities for teachers and staff to be involved in policy development • Involves school leadership team in decision making
Intellectual Stimulation	.32	. . . ensures that faculty and staff are aware of the most current theories and practices and makes the discussion of these a regular aspect of the school's culture.	• Stays informed about current research and theory regarding effective schooling • Continually exposes teachers and staff to cutting edge ideas about how to be effective • Systematically engages teachers and staff in discussions about current research and theory • Continually involves teachers and staff in reading articles and books about effective practices

(Continued)

Table 12.1 (Continued)

Responsibility	Definition: The Extent to Which the Principal . . .	Average r	Associated Practices
Knowledge of Curriculum, Instruction, Assessment	. . . is knowledgeable about current curriculum, instruction, and assessment practices.	.24	• Is knowledgeable about curriculum and instructional practices • Is knowledgeable about assessment practices • Provides conceptual guidance for teachers regarding effective classroom practice
Monitors/Evaluates	. . . monitors the effectiveness of school practices and their impact on student learning.	.28	• Monitors and evaluates the effectiveness of the curriculum • Monitors and evaluates the effectiveness of instruction • Monitors and evaluates the effectiveness of assessment
Optimizer	. . . inspires and leads new and challenging innovations.	.20	• Inspires teachers and staff to accomplish things that might seem beyond their grasp • Portrays a positive attitude about the ability of teachers and staff to accomplish substantial things • Is a driving force behind major initiatives
Order	. . . establishes a set of standard operating principles and procedures.	.26	• Provides and enforces clear structures, rules, and procedures for teachers, staff, and students • Establishes routines regarding the running of the school that teachers and staff understand and follow • Ensures that the school is in compliance with district and state mandates
Outreach	. . . is an advocate or spokesperson for the school to all stakeholders.	.28	• Advocates on behalf of the school in the community • Interacts with parents in ways that enhance their support for the school • Ensures that the central office is aware of the school's accomplishments

		r	
Relationships	. . . demonstrates an awareness of the personal aspects of teachers and staff.	.19	• Remains aware of personal needs of teachers and staff • Maintains personal relationships with teachers and staff • Is informed about significant personal issues in the lives of teachers and staff • Acknowledges significant events in the lives of teachers and staff
Resources	. . . provides teachers with the material and professional development necessary for the successful execution of their jobs.	.26	• Ensures that teachers and staff have necessary materials and equipment • Ensures that teachers have necessary professional development opportunities that directly enhance their teaching
Situational Awareness	. . . is aware of the details and undercurrents on the running of the school and uses this information to address current potential problems.	.33	• Is aware of informal groups and relationships among teachers and staff • Is aware of issues in the school that have not surfaced but could create discord • Can predict what could go wrong from day to day
Visibility	. . . has quality contact and interactions with teachers and students.	.16	• Makes systematic and frequent visits to classrooms • Is highly visible around the school • Has frequent contact with students

SOURCE: Waters, T., & Grubb, S. (2004). *The Leadership we need: Using research to strengthen the use of standards for administrator preparation and licensure programs.* Denver, CO: Mid-Continent Research for Education and Learning. Copyright 2004. Reprinted by permission of McREL.

NOTE: The *r* correlations reported in this table were derived from McREL's leadership meta-analysis.

(*Text continued from page 114*)

Excellence, referenced in earlier chapters of this book, described eight principles of leadership in "America's best run companies." These were as follows:

1. A bias for action
2. Close to the customer
3. Autonomy and entrepreneurship
4. Productivity through people
5. Hands on, value driven
6. Stick to the knitting
7. Simple form, lean staff
8. Simultaneous loose-tight properties

Peters and Waterman used an approach resembling the approach Collins (2001) used when they identified the very successful companies; the criteria they used were also very similar.

We noticed that many of the activities and behaviors described by Collins (2001) paralleled the leadership principles set forth by Peters and Waterman ([1982] 2004) 19 years earlier. Table 12.2 compares the attributes of great CEOs presented in *Good to Great* with the leadership principles operative in America's best-run companies as portrayed in the book *In Search of Excellence.*

Notice that Collins' (2001) hedgehog concept is reminiscent of the sticking to one's knitting recommended by Peters and Waterman. In addition, reading about simultaneously loose-tight organizations reminds us of the culture of discipline discussions, and so forth.

Table 12.2   Relating Collins' (2001) Leader Behaviors to Peters and Waterman's ([1982] 2004) Principles of Leadership

Collins' Leader Behaviors	Peters and Waterman's Principles
"First Who . . . Then What"	Productivity Through People
	Simple Form, Lean Staff
Confront the Brutal Facts	A Bias for Action
The Hedgehog Concept	Stick to Knitting
	Close to the Customer
A Culture of Discipline	Simultaneous Loose-Tight Properties
	Autonomy and Entrepreneurship
	Hands-On, Value Driven

BEWARE OF BUSINESS NORMS

Many of us who have spent parts of our careers in the private sector know that much can be learned from business leaders. We also recognize that much of what has been done in the management of education is often superior to the private sector. In his recent publication, *Good to Great in the Social Sectors*, Collins admitted, "We must reject the idea—well intentioned, but dead wrong—that the primary path to greatness in the social sectors is to become 'more like business'" (2005, p. 1).

Business norms are not the path to greatness for public schools, but the principles of great leadership are. Moreover, the evidence suggests that these principles of great leadership are linked to increased student performance—the fundamental mission of the public schools.

ADMINISTRATOR PREPARATION PROGRAM REFORM

An administrator preparation program curriculum consisting of heavy doses of school law, school finance, human resources management, leadership principles, and curriculum management is comfortable and defensible. After all, most practicing administrators would agree that a working knowledge of the laws governing schools is important. We thought so, and, to a large extent, we still do. We continue to believe these knowledge bases are important, but we are convinced there is much more.

Our study of highly successful principals was small and, therefore, cannot be considered conclusive. More research focused on these leadership behaviors and characteristics must be conducted before solid conclusions are drawn. However, our research suggests that Collins' (2001) work in *Good to Great* is right on target as an approach for deciding what school administrators should really know. The focus of a principal preparation program should be on developing leadership behaviors and characteristics that are typical of exemplary principals and that have an impact on the success of schools. In other words, the program should concentrate on how great school leaders behave and what they do to make a difference. This requires that we embrace the premise that research-based determinants should replace the old consensus-based standards. Otherwise, we are stuck in the status quo, or worse, doomed to become part of the profit-oriented private sector and surrender our traditional role supporting American democracy in its quest for social justice.

ISLLC Standards and Social Justice

Recently, Fenwick English (2005) attacked the whole notion of the ISLLC standards. "To specify in advance the range of objectives that are required to perform a job requires one to freeze it. When the duties are fixed to a role that is fixed, the school and the society in which it functions *must also be fixed*"(p. 9, emphasis in original). English makes a strong case that the ISLLC standards are based in a socially static view of schools and society. They reinforce the status quo. "And in this mixture the social order is also fixed, *as it is*" (p. 10, emphasis in original). Not long ago, the National Council for the Accreditation of Teacher Education embraced the ISLLC product. Since the Council provides accreditation for most of the administrator preparation programs, the program designers for the colleges (and for the states, for that matter) are under intense pressure to buy all the standards and include them in their program design guidelines. Mighty strong leverage!

Reforming Preparation Programs for Ed Leadership

So what does all this mean to school administrator preparation programs? For one, it means the colleges and universities, above all, must develop educational leaders who tackle the unique challenges of their institutions and strive to achieve greatness. We agree this sounds like a big order, but it must be done. We must also improve the image of administrator preparation programs. When we asked our highly successful principals about their preparation programs, they were generally lukewarm in their responses.

Mr. Bond: On the positive side, it was one of relationships and networking, not the actual course work or program or the jumping through hoops and watching each of us go in different ways. And [allowing] those of us who became area principals and administrators to be able to call and say, "Hey! How are things going?" On the negative side, we never looked at what the research was saying. We weren't doing that. For example, what does the research say about faculty meetings? I never read about that in my course materials.

Mr. Bond is typical of many administrators who mention the social aspect with its networking possibilities as the most valuable part of the preparation program. One wonders if they think a bowling league would be just as effective for training principals.

The use of practicing administrators to teach the courses was frequently cited as a plus, especially in classes taught in traditional lecture fashion. Administrators on the job are viewed as being in touch. And if the mission of a program is to prepare administrators to support the status quo, then this practice makes a lot of sense.

Fixing Our School Leadership Programs

Most of us recognize that not every person can be educated to be a great leader, but our preparation programs must be designed to give a fighting chance to those who have what it takes. Many practicing administrators complain that the programs currently in existence are simply hurdles to be jumped, dues to be paid—in fact, detriments to recruiting the stars we need to lead schools to greatness. What, then, are the implications for program improvement resulting from the research and professional dialogue we have just concluded? Our study suggests program modifications are called for in two categories, pedagogy and curriculum, as follows.

Pedagogy

1. *Incorporate Mentors Throughout.* Probably the most universally positive responses were related to mentors. Comments from our highly successful principals offered insight:

Mr. Bond:	Harry Goodman was and is my mentor. It was his pearls of wisdom. I first met him in 1983 when I was becoming a member of the local PDK [Phi Delta Kappa]. He was my sponsor. I appreciate that he always looks for the good in what is to become.
Mr. Unpretentious:	A principal convinced me to come here. We used to meet every single week for breakfast and talk about things related to school and how to handle it.
Ms. Persevere:	My district mentor was someone I could call. I admire her and our styles are similar. She is just a phone call away. We mentor each other. We would debrief the day and share experiences.
Ms. Aspiration:	The assistant superintendent for our district. He pushed me to be an administrator. He made me realize that I could make a difference as an administrator. He really stressed and believed in staff development, even if it meant being out of class. I could still go to him today if I needed advice.
Mr. Focus:	Glen Serious was my mentor. Glen was a principal I worked for and then was assistant superintendent when I was the curriculum coordinator. Glen modeled what I believe: "Treat people professionally and support them in what they feel is important." He was a great guy. He taught me about how to budget, too, and use money wisely.
Ms. Discipline:	The former superintendent had faith in me and gave me the support I needed.

In both the private and public sector circles, mentoring has been credited with two benefits: first, mentoring is an effective career development and management training tool for employees; second, mentoring offers a number of organizational benefits such as retention of quality employees, effective succession planning, and increased organizational commitment.

2. *Emphasize Field Experience Throughout.* Some elements in the principal preparation programs fared better in the principal interviews than others—most notably the field experience. This aspect of the preparation program was simply deemed very practical and relevant. Most of the candidates reported positive reactions to the field experience. One commented, "The practicum was the most meaningful [part of the program]."

In the course of a study of principals across the country (Portin, Schneider, DeArmond, & Gundlach, 2003), principals discussed their credential programs and the experiences that best prepared them for school leadership. Regardless of their training, most principals thought they learned the skills they needed "on the job" (p. 37). The closest thing to on-the-job training in administrative preparation preservice is field experience.

We recognize that field experiences may differ widely. Some are tightly connected to the formal course curriculum and serve as a lab for classroom theory. Others are less coordinated. As a result of our conversations with the principals, tempered by our extensive practical experience, we favor careful integration of coursework and fieldwork. This requires a well-coordinated team approach to the classroom and field programs. It's more work, but well worth it. Nevertheless, regardless of the program design, our candidates made a strong case for the hands-on fieldwork aspect. They felt it was valuable—and so do we.

3. *Use a Problem-Based Approach.* The problem-based approach to administrator preparation presents the opportunity for talented candidates to investigate, research, and learn in the well-proven hands-on mode. Valuable guidance for developing this approach is available in the literature (Bridges & Hallinger, 1992). Organizing and coordinating a problem-based approach is time consuming. It requires much advance class preparation. The results, though, are very positive. The candidates are far more engaged. Most important, with the proper professor guidance, they are learning and practicing the right things—the behaviors that, as our research tells us, coalesce to produce *great* principals.

4. *Concentrate on Research.* Many of our graduates have second-class educations devoid of refined research skills and lacking in the scholarly background necessary to become the academic leaders needed in great schools. We at the university have allowed this to happen. The excuse? We must compete for candidates. If we demand rigorous academic research, they will go somewhere else. This sort of thinking is purely wrong headed. If the programs really make a difference, candidates will seek the superior

preparation. As a former superintendent and curriculum director, we valued well-prepared personnel and avoided the candidates looking for shortcuts. Most of the successful school leaders we know agree.

Preparation Program Curriculum

1. *Eliminate the Myths.* In other words, exalt empirical evidence as a basis for administrative action. Spend hands-on time collecting information and deciding how to use it. Throughout history, myths have been used to prop up the status quo. Course curriculum in the preparation of school leaders should include rigorous examination of the axioms and truths we build our schools around—from state and national testing to grouping and grading, and from teacher evaluation to school size (Frase & Streshly, 2000).

2. *Teach the Necessary Human Relations Skills.* Prominent among the behaviors of our highly successful principals was the demonstrated ability to build strong human relationships. Contrary to popular opinion, human relations skills can be *taught.* The counselor preparation departments have been doing it for years. They call it counseling practicum, and counselor candidates are taught how to relate to clients individually and in groups. Not every candidate will catch on, but the talented ones will—and they deserve a program that emphasizes this critical leadership skill.

3. *Study Great Leaders.* This is where we began. A program whose goal is to prepare great leaders must focus on what great leaders do. The coursework should include study of such men as Niccolò Machiavelli and Abraham Lincoln, as well as examples of principals whose schools made the leap from good to great. This idea is not new. We have been educating our military leaders this way since wars were first fought. It's time to use this technique to strengthen our frontline school leaders.

A FINAL COMMENT

The core of our research for this book focused on a small number of outstanding school principals. Students of leadership have long recognized that one must study great leaders in order to truly learn about great leadership. Five hundred years ago, Machiavelli advised the leaders of his day to consider the virtue and discipline of the finest leaders of the past in order to identify the most worthy character traits. He then admonished them to imitate the ancients. Today, business leaders have come to realize clearly the essential role of the personal forces of leadership in shaping the destinies of our nation's business enterprises. Today's school leaders also recognize these dynamics. The result has been a renewed effort to equip school administrators with powerful leadership expertise.

From our interviews, we learned our star principals have much in common with the star CEOs in the private sector studied by Jim Collins. We also noticed that, although they were very different personalities, all of the great school leaders in our study placed a high degree of importance on building relationships among the members of their staffs—and they were good at it! We weren't surprised. Schooling is almost entirely a human relations enterprise. It makes sense that the leader of such an enterprise would be expert at fostering productive interpersonal relations among its members. Moreover, a close examination of the personal qualities and behaviors that we observed among our principals, such as those the Collins (2001) researchers observed among the CEOs, reveals they are all, in the final analysis, aspects of relationships among human beings.

At the beginning of Chapter 1 we asked the question, "We know what to do, so why do we fail?" The answer, simply, is some of our school leaders are equipped to lead, but others aren't. The *Good to Great* research has shed light on personal aspects of leadership that distinguish our outstanding business leaders. Our study strongly suggests that the *Good to Great* research is also applicable to school leaders. This has enormous implications for improving the preparation of school administrators. The recommendations for fixing our administrator preparation programs we make in this chapter are products of our three-year research project. They are intended to encourage further discussion in the continuous effort to improve administrator preparation.

The interview methodology implemented first in the Collins (2001) research of *Good to Great* companies and subsequently in our study of a small number of successful school principals certainly has merit for principal preparation. Interview questions such as ours could be used to help aspiring principals identify their own and others' strengths and areas for growth. Problem-based learning projects and case studies could be developed from data collected through interviews and analyzed by leadership students to better understand those characteristics and behaviors common to highly successful principals. We have made a case in this book that building relationships is a key skill needed for successful school leadership. Students studying case studies of successful principals could better grasp how these different leaders go about building relationships. The time has come to rethink our administrator preparation programs to focus more attention on the personal forces of leadership.

REFLECTION

Assume you are responsible for the design of a new principal preparation program. How would you approach this task? What guiding principles would you embrace? What resources would you need to accomplish your design project? What would you need to accomplish your delivery mission?

SUGGESTIONS FOR ARCHITECTS OF
PRINCIPAL PREPARATION PROGRAMS

- Redesign the principal preparation program to place more emphasis on human relations aspects of school administration. Teach the characteristics of the Level 5 leader. Do as Machiavelli suggested and imitate the ancients.

- Use the knowledge bases developed to support training in counseling and guidance to enhance the interpersonal skills of principal candidates. Require principal candidates to participate in clinical counseling practicums to develop skills associated with building relationships.

- Provide candidates with an understanding of the importance of establishing and maintaining personal relationships with a wide range of staff members.

- Give the candidates hands-on, problem-based projects focused on developing, strengthening, and nurturing collaborative, problem-solving teachers and staff. Make these problem-based projects the core of a carefully focused field experience or internship.

- Equip candidates with strategies for surveying faculty and staff to determine professional concerns. Provide them with techniques to establish and execute plans to address the concerns with the highest priority.

- Include strategies and techniques for working with a school's faculty and staff to design and implement systems for celebrating successes, at the same time acknowledging evidence of weaknesses, shortcomings, or failures.

- Prepare principal candidates with strategies and techniques for involving large numbers of teachers in planning and organizing instructional improvement including curriculum development and program assessment. Equip them with the knowledge and special skills necessary to create a faculty and staff who are self-diagnosing, auto-correcting, and self-renewing.

- Assist the candidates to plan daily and weekly calendars to include frequent classroom walk-throughs and informal contact with students.

- Emphasize the importance of reaching out to the community through strong support of parent groups and active involvement in the community.

- Finally, don't eliminate altogether the traditional law, finance, leadership, and curriculum studies—just abbreviate them. Principals need to understand the legal, political, financial, and technical aspects of their jobs, but a hard look at outcomes tells us that this alone will not result in great principals or great schools.

Resource A

Research Methodology

SEMISTRUCTURED QUALITATIVE INTERVIEW

This exploration was a qualitative study that included description, interpretation, understanding, and identification of recurrent patterns, as described by Merriam (1998). Collins (2001) and his researchers collected information by using a variety of methods. However, central to their examination of the leadership in the 11 *Good to Great* companies were open-ended qualitative interviews. The intent here was to replicate those interviews (as modified to apply to school leadership) with a group of principals whose schools moved from good to great in student achievement, and a group of comparison principals whose schools were good but did not move to great. Collins named the CEOs of the *Good to Great* companies *Level 5 Executives*. For purposes of this study, the name given to the principals of the schools that moved from good to great in student achievement was *highly successful principals*.

The interview is probably the most widely used method of qualitative research. The flexibility of the qualitative research interview makes it attractive for purposes of this exploration as opposed to the rigidity of quantitative study. In this study, as in Collins' (2001) research, there is an emphasis on the interviewee's own perspectives and points of view. This is a process of finding patterns in the stories of the principals interviewed.

One of the powerful aspects of Collins' research is that it "zeros out systemic factors vs. whining factors" (2004). The leaders of Collins' *Good to Great* companies and comparison companies all faced constraints outside their control. Similarly the highly successful and comparison principals in this study faced constraints such as union problems, hiring and firing restrictions, chronic personnel issues, and the diversity of the student population. Nonetheless, just as the *Good to Great* companies were able to outperform other similar companies, students of *Good to Great* schools were able to outperform students of other schools with similar demographics. People can often make breakthroughs despite those systemic factors.

The interview process was semistructured. By using semistructured interviews, the interviewer collected a richer understanding of the information collected (Smith, 1995). These interviews were conducted with an open framework allowing for focused, conversational, two-way communication. The interview was guided by a series of questions that are modifications of the questions asked of CEOs in Collins' (2001) research (see Resource C for Principal Interview Questions). As each interview progressed, participants were encouraged to raise additional or complementary issues relevant to the study's purposes. In addition, lines of thought identified by earlier interviewees were taken up and presented to later interviewees in second interviews for refinement of ideas. By using open-ended, semistructured interviews, we could explore what the interviewee saw as relevant and important (McCracken, 1988).

DEMOGRAPHIC INFORMATION QUESTIONNAIRE AND INTERVIEW PROCEDURES

Collins' (2001) researchers examined 56 CEOs via interview and document analysis for (1) management style, (2) executive persona, (3) personal life, and (4) each one's top five priorities as CEO. Demographic information was collected for each for background and tenure information. The same method was replicated with modifications for this study of principals in successful schools using the semistructured qualitative interview method and a demographic information questionnaire (see Resource C). Questions to guide the interview were based on those asked in Collins' research, but with modification to be applicable to school leadership. Additional questions were added as necessary to extract more comprehensive information concerning the characteristics and behaviors of the principals. In addition, questions were added to look at life and educational experiences influencing the leadership of the principals interviewed. The demographic information questionnaire and principal interview questions were piloted with a principal who did not participate in the formal study. Questions were refined further based on the results of the pilot. The one- to two-hour interviews were conducted in private, in a location selected by each interviewee. All but one of the principal interviews were conducted in the principal's office at his or her school. One of the principals in the comparison group was interviewed at her home at her request. Before beginning the interview, principals were asked to complete the demographic information questionnaire. Notes were taken during the interview on a laptop computer, and the interview was tape recorded as back-up for the notes. Principals were contacted by telephone when clarification or additional information was warranted subsequent to the interview.

DATA ANALYSIS PROCEDURES

The participants' names, school names, and district names were kept confidential by using fictitious names. The records of this study were kept private; the researcher was the only person who had access to the original records. Immediately following each interview, the computer notes were compared with the taped responses to ensure all information had been recorded.

The original responses to interview questions and data from the demographic information questionnaire for each participant were entered into ATLAS.ti qualitative analysis software. The responses for all participants were coded using the tools of the software. Categories for the first round of coding were based on an analysis of the responses in relation to Collins' (2001) characteristics and behaviors of a Level 5 Executive. For example, we asked the following question: "What do you see as the top five factors that have contributed to the success in student achievement performance at the school?" One factor volunteered by a interviewee was "We all decided as a group to implement a new reading program at Grades 1–3. In the first year, we saw gains in student test scores. My teachers should be credited for that . . . and maybe [it was] a little [bit of] luck too!" Aspects of this statement were coded as consistent with Collins' definition of compelling modesty. The second round of coding was expanded to include additional characteristics and behaviors generated by the interviewee (e.g., shared decision making, building relationships, visiting classrooms, trust). The earlier question and response example received an additional code of shared decision making. During the coding process, additional ideas generated from the questions asked—or by ideas volunteered from the interviewee—materialized, and coding was refined further to explore patterns among the principals interviewed relevant to the study. Related codes were grouped together in code families. Table A.1 presents the code families applied in this analysis.

As noted in Table A.1, code family headings were the characteristics and behaviors that Collins (2001) identified in his Level 5 Executives. One additional code family heading was "building relationships." As the principal responses were coded, notes were made to clarify reasons for the coding. The refined coding of the responses served to organize the data, interpretations, and connections to existing literature, analysis, and conclusions of the study.

Table A.1   Code Families

Code Family	Related Codes
Duality of Professional Will and Personal Humility	Acts as a Screen Humble Fearless Catalyst
Ambition for Success of Company	School First Encourages Professionalism Promotes Leadership Puts Value on Staff Development Concern for Successor
Compelling Modesty	Gives Credit Self-Effacing Understated Takes Blame Supports Teachers
Unwavering Resolve	Relentless Determined Persuasive Aggressive Persistent Has a Classroom Presence
"First Who . . . Then What"	Authority to Hire Latitude to Hire and Fire Selective Persistent in Getting People
Confront the Brutal Facts	Analyzes Data Works Through Problems Not Resigned
The Hedgehog Concept	Passionate Knows What Can Be Best At Knows What Will Make the Difference
Culture of Discipline	Vision Not Micromanager Focuses on Student Achievement Respects Teacher Freedom
Building Relationships	People Skills Open-Door Policy Communication Staff Involvement Shared Decision Making Teachers Working Together

SOURCE: Adapted from Collins (2001).

Resource B

Interview Participant Selection

The intent here was to study the characteristics and behaviors of highly successful principals, and not of the schools themselves. Therefore, a measure of success was needed. Criterion for selection of the subjects in the study is student test performance, specifically the California Academic Performance Index (API). Student test performance is affected by many demographic factors that are not under the control of a principal. In order to eliminate as many of those factors as possible, the API similar school ranking system is used. In the similar school ranking system, schools are compared to schools with like demographics such as mobility, credentialed teachers, language, average class size, multitrack year-round schedule, ethnicity, and free or reduced price meals. It is important to note here that the schools in this study were not in the same similar schools comparison groups. These data are presented in Table B.1.

The data presented in Table B.1 suggest that certain demographics of the schools may affect the success of a school. For example, there may be a positive relationship between year-round school configurations and the success of the school, and the percentage of English language learners may be a barrier to success as measured by student test scores. However, the State of California's API formula gave a certain weight to each of the demographics and did not weight these factors as important as others in determining API similar schools rank for schools. Each school's school characteristic index (SCI), a composite of the school's demographic characteristics, is calculated. Then a comparison group for each school is formed by placing the school's SCI as the median, and taking the 50 schools with SCIs just above the median and the 50 just below the median. Principals in these 100 similar schools have similar issues with which to contend. The 100 schools are sorted from lowest to highest according to their API base, then are divided into 10 equal-sized groups (deciles). Schools with a decile of 9 or 10 in rank are doing qualitatively better than the other 100 schools in their demographic group. For purposes of this exploration, 14 San Diego, Riverside,

Table B.1   School Demographics

Highly Successful Schools	*Mountain High*	*Mission*	*Field*	*Pines*	*Bay View*	*Eagle*
Year-Round Status 1999	No	No	No	Yes	Yes	Yes
Year-Round Status 2003	Yes	No	No	Yes	Yes	No
Grade Span	K–5	K–5	K–5	K–5	K–6	K–5
Enrollment	479	757	426	911	729	630
Ethnicity						
White (%)	48.9	26.4	54.5	36.3	14	69.2
Hispanic (%)	24.1	56.5	19.7	53	65	15.9
African American (%)	8	6.9	15.7	1.9	3.6	6.0
Other (%)	18.0	10.3	10.1	4	17	8.2
Percent English language learners	12.2	29.7	.5	39.8	31	4.8
Percent Free or Reduced Price Meal Eligibility	28.2	51.7	40.6	51.1	43	4.9

Comparison Schools	*Elm*	*Roosevelt*	*Observatory*	*Sunkist*	*Johnson*
Year-Round Status 1999	No	No	No	Yes	No
Year-Round Status 2003	No	No	No	Yes	No
API 2001	6	9	10	3	7
API 2002	8	8	6	5	9
API 2003	7	7	4	7	8
Grade Span	K–6	K–6	K–6	K–5	K–5
Enrollment	585	502	438	666	1,027
Ethnicity					
White (%)	55.4	7.2	12.1	4.7	7.1
Hispanic (%)	31.1	27.3	78.5	31.7	81.6

(Continued)

Table B.1 (Continued)

Comparison Schools	Elm	Roosevelt	Observatory	Sunkist	Johnson
African American (%)	10.6	1.2	3.9	46.7	1.3
Other (%)	2.9	1.8	5.4	17.1	9.8
Asian (Vietnamese) (%)	—	62.5	—	—	—
Percent English language learners	22.6	57.6	29	21.8	58.2
Percent Free or Reduced Price Meal Eligibility	64.5	54.8	57.3	74.6	72.4

SOURCE: Data from California Department of Education Web site, Academic Performance Index Reports (http://api.cde.ca.gov/reports.asp) and Ed-Data (http://www.ed-data.k12.ca.us/welcome.asp)

and Orange County school principals were identified initially. From those initial 14, 11 agreed to participate and three declined. Six of the 11 participants were identified as highly successful principals. The five remaining participants were identified in the study as comparison principals.

Selection of the highly successful principals was based on the following criteria:

- The principal's school had a sustained California API similar schools rank of 9 or 10 in 2001, 2002, and 2003. The rank of 9 or 10 is considered by California Department of Education as "well-above average" or "highly successful." In 1999, the school's similar schools rank was two or more deciles lower than in 2001, but no lower than a 5. (The rank of 5, 6, 7, or 8 is considered by California Department of Education as "above average" or "good.") The purpose here was to choose schools that had moved from "good" to "highly successful" in student achievement over the five years in the study. In addition, there had been no significant change in demographics at the school during the five-year period that might skew the test results (as noted in interviews or the school academic report). Ranking and demographic information was obtained on the California Department of Education Web site.
- The school ranked in decile 4 or higher in both 1999 and 2003 in relative rank. In this relative ranking, a school's API is compared to all other schools in the state.

- The principals of the chosen schools had been at the school for the entire time (1999 through 2003). This information was obtained directly from the central office of the district in which the principal worked and by reference to the *California Public School Directories* for the years 2000 through 2003.

This study explored commonalities shared by highly successful principals. In order to see if these shared characteristics are different from those of other principals, a comparison group of principals was identified. The difference between the schools headed by principals in the comparison group and the schools headed by principals in the highly successful group is the sustained nature of each school's success. The comparison principals' schools started at a similar level to the highly successful principals' schools in 1999 with an API similar school rank of "above average" or "good," but were unable to move to "well-above average" or "highly successful" and sustain that success. The primary criteria for the selection of principals in the comparison group are the following three:

1. In 1999, the school's similar schools rank was no lower than a 5 and no higher than an 8 (i.e., above average or good).

2. Subsequent ranks for 2000 through 2003 remained the same or fluctuated.

3. The principals of the chosen schools had been at the school for the entire period 1999 through 2003.

The purpose of the study is to compare the characteristics shared by highly successful principals to the characteristics of principals heading schools that did not sustain success. However, in an effort to reduce as much as feasible the variables that might affect that success, the study also sought to identify schools that were as similar as possible. Therefore, principals in the highly successful group and principals in the comparison group were chosen where practical from their shared list of 100 similar schools. Direct comparison of individual principals between the two study groups was not intended in this study. This attempt to reduce variables between schools was partially successful. Four of the comparison principals headed schools that were in the same 100 similar schools lists as the highly successful principals. In a fifth case, a comparison principal was interviewed, but the highly successful principal from the same similar schools list did not ultimately participate. This comparison principal remained in the study because she still met the primary criteria for being included in the comparison group. In the last case, one highly successful principal in the study did participate but all of the potential comparison principals from the same 100 similar schools list declined to participate. Once again, because the intent was not to compare individual principals, this was not a serious obstacle to the study. In all, a total study set of 11 principals, six highly successful principals and five comparison principals, participated in the study.

The project, along with other required materials, conformed to the Claremont Graduate University (CGU) *Procedures for the Review of Research Protocols* and the San Diego State University (SDSU) *Human Research Protection Program: Guidance, Standards and Practices.* Individual principal participation was solicited only after both CGU and SDSU Institutional Review Board approvals were received.

Principals were initially invited through e-mail to participate in the study and given background information, significance of the study, and procedures for participation. All 11 principals were told that the criteria used to select them for the study was based on their API similar schools ranks from 1999 through 2003 and the fact that they were principals of the school for the entire time. They were not informed that there were two groups being studied, that is, highly successful principals and comparison principals. They were informed that they were under no obligation to answer any questions and that at any point they could stop or withdraw from the interview. They were assured that the records of the study would be kept private and that all responses to the interview questions were confidential. All six of the highly successful principals responded positively to the e-mail; we followed up their responses with a phone call to their school to schedule the first interview. The comparison principals were more reticent to participate. In every case, their initial reason for declining or hesitating to participate was that they were too busy at that time. A follow-up phone call by the authors or a research advisor assured them that participation on their part was important for the study and that the interview could be scheduled at their convenience. Ultimately, five of the initial eight principals in the comparison group either phoned or e-mailed and agreed to participate. Before the beginning of the interview, all participants signed a form giving their consent to participate in the study.

Resource C

Principal Interview Questions Derived From Collins' (2001) CEO Interview Questions and Demographic Questionnaire

PRINCIPAL INTERVIEW QUESTIONS

1. Briefly, give me an overview of your relationship to the district, years in the district and at the school, and primary jobs held in the district.

2. Give me a brief description of the demographics of the school. Students? Community?

3. Tell me a little about the staff of the school in 1999 [first year of the API].

4. Why do you believe you were selected as principal of the school?

5. What kind of leadership style do you think you have?

6. What kind of leadership style would your teachers say you have?

7. I'd like you to take a minute and write down the top five factors that you believe have contributed to the school's success in improving student achievement performance at the school. [Give interviewee a piece of paper.]

8. Now number them in order of importance with 1 being the most important factor.

9. Talk a little about the [top two or three] factors that you listed. Give me some examples that illustrate the factors.

10. What decision did the school make to initiate an increase in student achievement during the years prior [1997–1999?] to receiving a ranking of 9 or 10 on the 2000 API? What sparked that decision?

11. What role did technology play in all this?

12. What latitude did you have as principal of the school to make the decisions you had to make? In what ways were you restricted?

13. What process did you and the school staff use to make key decisions and develop key strategies that led to the increase in student achievement performance at the school? [Not what decisions the school made, but how did it go about making them?]

14. On a scale or 1 to 10, what confidence did you have in the decisions at the time they were made, before you knew their outcome? [10: you had great confidence that they were very good decisions with high probability of success; 1: you had little confidence in the decisions; they seemed risky—a roll of the dice.] [If interviewee had confidence of 6 or greater: What gave you such confidence in the decisions?]

15. What was the role, if any, of outside consultants, advisors, and central office personnel in making the key decisions?

16. How did the school get commitment and agreement with its decisions from everyone? Teachers, parents, students? Give me a specific example of how this took place.

17. What did you do to ensure that teachers continued to focus on improving student test performance?

18. What did you try that didn't work during the years before attaining a similar schools ranking of 9 or 10? Why didn't it work?

19. How did your school manage the pressures of district, state, and federal accountability while making these long-term changes for the future?

20. Many schools undertake change programs and initiatives, yet their efforts do not produce lasting results. One of the remarkable aspects of [Successful School's] transition is that it endured over several years, and was not just a short-term upswing. We find this extraordinary. What makes [Successful School] different? What were the primary factors in maintaining the similar schools ranking over the years?

21. Tell me about one particularly powerful example or vignette from your experience or observation that, to you, exemplifies the essence of the success at [Successful School].

22. I'd like to switch gears a bit here. Talk to me a bit about the administrative credential preparation courses you have taken. On a scale of 1 to 5 how would you rate them? [1: of value; 5: of great value]. [If 3 or more: Give me a few examples of elements of your course work that you believe to be of value to the work you do as a principal.]

23. Whom do you consider to be your mentor(s)? Talk to me about that person(s) and why he or she is your mentor.

24. Talk to me about some experience related to work or to your personal life or experience that you have had in the past that you believe helped to shape your leadership.

25. What did you do to ensure that teachers continued to focus on improving student test performance?

26. What do or did you want most for your school?

27. When you think about your work here, what are you most proud of?

28. What efforts do or did you make to ensure that the school continued to sustain its success?

29. When you leave your position as principal, what do you want to be remembered for?

30. What else would you like to tell me about the reasons for the success of your school in raising student achievement?

DEMOGRAPHIC QUESTIONNAIRE

Circle your responses.

1. Were you brought in from outside the district *directly* into the principal position at the school?
   a. Yes
   b. No

2. Length of employment in the school district before becoming principal of the school:
   a. 10+ years
   b. 4–9 years
   c. 1–3 years
   d. Less than a year

3. Age at the time of becoming the principal of the school:
   a. Less than 25
   b. 25–30
   c. 31–40
   d. 41–50
   e. 51+

4. Length of tenure as the principal of the school:
   a. 7–10+ years
   b. 5–6 years
   c. 3–4 years

5. Job held immediately before becoming principal of the school:
   a. Principal
   b. Assistant principal
   c. Teacher
   d. Other administrator
   e. Other

6. Where did you receive administrative credential? (select one):
   a. California
   b. Other state
   c. Other country
      What institution? _____

7. Received master's degree in (select all that apply):
   a. Educational administration
   b. Education
   c. Other: _____

8. Received doctoral degree in (select all that apply):
   a. Educational administration
   b. Education
   c. Other: _____

9. Work experience and other experiences (e.g., military) before coming to public education (select all that apply):
   a. Military
   b. Sales
   c. Government
   d. Technology/business
   e. Other: _____

10. Total length of time employed as a teacher before becoming an administrator:
    a. 15+
    b. 10–14
    c. 4–9
    d. 1–3
    e. Less than 1 year

11. Jobs held while employed in the current district (select all that apply):
    a. Principal
    b. Assistant principal
    c. Teacher
    d. Other administrative position
    e. Other certificated position (not administrative)
    f. Noncertificated position

12. Jobs held while at the current school (select all that apply):
    a. Principal
    b. Assistant principal
    c. Teacher
    d. Other administrative position
    e. Other certificated position (not administrative)
    f. Noncertificated position

References

Allen, L., Glickman, C., & Hensley, F. (1998). *A search for accountability: The league of professional schools.* Paper presented at the Annual Meeting of the American Educational Research Association, San Diego, CA.

Andrews, R., & Soder, R. (1987). Principal leadership and student achievement. *Educational Leadership, 44,* (6), 9–11.

Andrews, R., Soder, R., & Jacoby, B. (1986, April). *Principals' roles, other in-school variables and academic achievement by ethnicity and SES.* Paper presented at the Annual Meeting of the American Educational Research Association, San Francisco, CA.

Asherman, I., Bing, J., & Laroche, L. (2000). Building trust across cultural boundaries. *Itap International.* (Article originally appeared in the May 2000 issue of *Regulatory Affairs Focus.*) Retrieved July 12, 2006, from http://www.itapintl.com/buildingtrust.htm.

Bennis, W. G. (1984). The four competencies of leadership. *Training and Development Journal* (August), 15–19.

Berlin, I. (1993). *The hedgehog and the fox.* Chicago: Elephant Paperbacks.

Blake, R. R., & McCanse, A. A. (1991). *Leadership dilemmas: Grid solutions.* Houston, TX: Gulf Publishing Company.

Blase, J. (1985). The socialization of teachers: An ethnographic study of factors contributing to rationalization of the teacher's instructional perspective. *Urban Education, 20*(3), 235–56.

Blase, J., & Blase, J. R. (1986). A qualitative analysis of sources of teacher stress: Consequences for performance. *American Educational Research Journal, 23*(1), 13–40.

Blase, J., & Blase, J. R. (1994). *Empowering teachers: What successful principals do.* Thousand Oaks, CA: Corwin Press.

Blase, J., & Kirby, P. (2000). *Bringing out the best in teachers: What effective principals do.* Thousand Oaks, CA: Corwin Press.

Blount, J. M. (1998). *Destined to rule the schools: Women and the superintendency.* Albany, NY: University of New York Press.

Blount, J. M. (1999). Turning out the ladies: Elected women superintendents and the push for the appointive system, 1900–1935. In C. C. Brunner (Ed.), *Sacred dreams: Women and the superintendency* (pp. 9–27). Albany: State University of New York Press.

Bridges, E., & Hallinger, P. (1992). *Problem-based learning for administrators.* Eugene, OR: ERIC Clearinghouse on Educational Management.

Brunard, V., & Kleiner, B. H. (1994). Developing trustful and cooperative relationships. *Leadership & Organization Development Journal, 15*(2), 3–5.

Bryk, A. S., & Schneider, B. L. (2002). *Trust in schools: A core resource for improvement.* New York: Russell Sage Foundation.

Chester, M., & Beaudin, B. (1996). Efficacy beliefs of newly hired teachers in urban schools. *American Educational Research Journal, 33*(1), 233–57.

Coch, L., & French, J. (1948). Overcoming resistance to change. *Human Relations, 1*(4), 512–32.

Coleman, J., Campbell, E., Bobson, C., McPartland, J., Mood, A., Weinfeld, F., et al. (1966). *Equality of educational opportunity.* Washington, DC: U.S. Government Printing Office.

Collins, J. (2001). *Good to great: Why some companies make the leap . . . and others don't.* New York: HarperCollins.

Collins, J. (2004). Being charismatic and wrong is a bad combination. Audio recording. Retrieved January 7, 2005, from http://www.jimcollins.com/hall/index.html.

Collins, J. (2005). Good to great and the social sectors: Why business thinking is not the answer. Monograph to accompany *Good to great: Why some companies make the leap . . . and others don't,* by Jim Collins (2001). Boulder, CO: Author.

Covey, S. (1989). *The seven habits of highly effective people: Restoring the character ethic.* New York: Simon & Schuster.

Cuban, L. (2006, February). Why can't schools be like businesses? *The School Administrator.* Retrieved May 6, 2006, from http://www.aasa.org/publications/saarticledetail.cfm.

Darling-Hammond, L. (1997). *The right to learn.* San Francisco: Jossey-Bass.

Davis, S., Darling-Hammond, L., LaPointe, M., & Meyerson, D. (2005). *School leadership study: Developing successful principals.* Stanford, CA: Stanford Educational Leadership Institute.

DeMoss, K. (2002). Leadership styles and high-stakes testing: Principals that make a difference. *Education and Urban Society, 35*(1), 111–32.

De Pree, M. (1989). *Leadership is an art.* New York: Bantam Doubleday Dell Publishing Group, Inc.

Drucker, P. (1954). *The practice of management.* New York: Harper and Row.

Drucker, P. (1968). *The age of discontinuity: Guidelines to our changing society.* New York: Harper and Row.

DuFour, R. (2005). What is a professional learning community? In R. DuFour, R. Eaker, & R. DuFour (Eds.), *On common ground: The power of professional learning communities* (pp. 31–43). Bloomington, IN: Solution Tree.

DuFour, R., Eaker, R., & DuFour, R. (Eds.). (2005). *On common ground: The power of professional learning communities.* Bloomington, IN: Solution Tree.

English, W. F. (2005, June). Educational leadership for sale: Social justice, the ISLLC standards and the corporate assault on public schools. Paper presented at the 8th Annual Advanced Auditing Seminar, Big Sky, MT.

Fountas, I., & Pinnell, G. (1996). *Guided reading: Good first teaching for all children.* Portsmouth, NH: Heineman.

Frase, L. (1998). *An examination of teachers' flow experiences, efficacy, and instructional leadership in large inner-city school districts.* Paper presented at the Annual Meeting of American Educational Research Association, San Diego, CA.

Frase, L. (2003, April). *Policy implications for school work environments: Implications from a causal model regarding frequency of teacher flow experiences, school principal classroom walk-through visits, teacher evaluation and professional development, and efficacy measures.* Paper presented at the Annual Meeting of American Educational Research Association, Chicago, IL.

Frase, L., & Streshly, W. (2000). *The top ten myths in education: Fantasies Americans love to believe about their schools.* Lanham, MD: Scarecrow Press.

Frase, L., Zhu, N., & Galloway, F. (2001, April). *An examination of the relationships among principal classroom visits, teacher flow experiences, and student cognitive engagement in two inner-city school districts.* Paper presented at the Annual Meeting of the American Educational Research Association, Seattle, WA.

Freedman, B., & Lafleur, C. (2002, April). *Making leadership visible and practical: Walking for improvement.* Paper presented at the Annual Meeting of the American Educational Research Association, New Orleans, LA.

Fullan, M. (1992). Visions that blind. *Educational Leadership, 49*(5), 19–20.

Fullan, M. (2001). *Leading in a culture of change.* San Francisco: Jossey-Bass.

Fullan, M. (2002). The change leader. *Educational Leadership, 59*(8), 16–20.

Fullan, M. (2003). *The moral imperative of school leadership.* Thousand Oaks, CA: Ontario Principals' Council/Corwin Press.

Fullan, M., & Hargreaves, A. (1991). *What's worth fighting for? Working together for your school.* Toronto: Ontario Public School Teachers' Federation.

Greenfield, W., & Blase, J. (1981). Motivating teachers: Understanding the factors that shape performance. *NASSP Bulletin, 65*(448), 1–10.

Hallinger, P., & Heck, R. (1996). Reassessing the principal's role in school effectiveness. *Educational Administration Quarterly, 32*(1), 5–44.

Heck, R., Larsen, T., & Marcoulides, G. (1990). Instructional leadership and school achievement: Validation of a causal model. *Educational Administration Quarterly, 26,* 94–125.

Hertzberg, F. (1959). *The motivation to work.* New York: John Wiley and Sons.

Houston, P. (2006, February). *Guess who's left behind?* Retrieved July 31, 2006, from http://www.aasa.org.

Kelleher, H. (1997). A culture of commitment. *Leader to Leader, 4* (Spring), 20–24. Retrieved July 15, 2006, from http://www.leadertoleader.org/knowledge center/L2L/spring97/kelleher.html

Keller, B. (1999). Women superintendents: Few and far between. *Education Week, 19*(11), 1.

Kim, S. (2002). Participative management and job satisfaction: Lessons for management leadership. *Public Administration Review, 62*(2), 231–41.

Kirkpatrick, S. A., & Locke, E. A. (1991). Leadership: Do traits matter? *Academy of Management Executive, 5*(2), 49–60.

Kouzes, J. M., & Posner, B. Z. (2002). *The leadership challenge* (3rd ed.). San Francisco: Jossey-Bass.

LaFee, S. (2004). Outside the ropes. *The School Administrator.* Retrieved July 9, 2006, from http://www.aasa.org/publications/saarticledetail.cfm?ItemNumber=1099.

Likert, R. (1967). *The human organization: Its management and value.* New York: McGraw-Hill.

Little, J. W. (1990). The persistence of privacy: Autonomy and initiative in teachers' professional relations. *Teachers' College Record, 91*(4), 509–36.

Louis, K., & Miles, M. (1990). *Improving the urban high school.* New York: Teachers College Press.

Maslow, A. H. (1943). A theory of human motivation. *Psychological Review, 50,* 370–96.

Matsui, B. (2002). *The Ysleta story: A tipping point in education.* Claremont, CA: The Institute at Indian Hill/CGU.

McCracken, G. (1988). *The long interview,* vol. 13, Qualitative Methods Series. Newbury Park, CA: SAGE.

McPherson, J. (1989). *Battle cry of freedom: The Civil War era.* New York: Ballantine Books.

Merriam, S. (1998). *Qualitative research and case study applications in research.* San Francisco: Jossey-Bass.

Merriam-Webster's Collegiate Dictionary. (2003). Springfield, MA: Merriam-Webster, Inc.

Murphy, J. T. (1988). The unheroic side of leadership: Notes from the swamp. *Phi Delta Kappan, 69*(9), 654–59.

Murphy, J. T. (2005). Unpacking the foundations of ISLLC standards and addressing concerns in the academic community. *Educational Administration Quarterly, 41*(1), 154–91.

Murphy, J. T., & Beck, L. (1994). Reclaiming a voice in discussions of the principal's role: A leadership challenge. In J. Murphy & K. Louis (Eds.), *Reshaping the principalship: Insights from transformational reform efforts.* Thousand Oaks, CA: Corwin Press.

Peters, T. J., & Waterman, R. H. (1982). *In search of excellence : Lessons from America's best-run companies.* Reprint (2004). New York: HarperBusiness Essentials.

Pfeffer, J., & Sutton, R. (2000). *The knowing-doing gap: How smart companies turn knowledge into action.* Boston: Harvard Business Press.

Portin, B., Schneider, P., DeArmond, M., & Gundlach, L. (2003). *Making sense of leading schools: A study of the school principalship.* A report prepared by the Center on Reinventing Public Education. Seattle: University of Washington.

Purkey, S. C., & Smith, M. S. (1983). Effective schools: A review. *The Elementary School Journal, 83*(4), 427–52.

Reeves, D. (2000). *Accountability in action: A Blueprint for learning* organizations, Denver, CO: Advanced Learning Centers, Inc.

Rubin, H. (2002). *Collaborative leadership: Developing effective partnerships in communities and schools.* Thousand Oaks, CA: Corwin Press.

Sagor, R. (1992). Three principals who make a difference. *Educational Leadership, 49*(5), 13–18.

Schmoker, M. (2005). No turning back: The ironclad case for professional learning communities. In R. DuFour, R. Eaker, & R. DuFour (Ed.), *On Common Ground: The power of professional learning communities* (pp. 135–154). Bloomington, IN: Solution Tree.

Schmoker, M. (2006). *Results Now: How we can achieve unprecedented improvements in teaching and learning.* Alexandria, VA: Association for Supervision and Curriculum Development.

Sergiovanni, T. J. (1992). On rethinking leadership: A conversation with Tom Sergiovanni. *Educational Leadership, 49*(5), 46–49.

Sergiovanni, T. J. (1996). *Leadership for the schoolhouse: How different is it?* San Francisco: Jossey-Bass.

Shields, C. (2004). Creating a community of difference. *Educational Leadership, 61*(7), 38–41.

Smith, J. (1995). Semi-structured interviewing and qualitative analysis. In J. Smith, R. Harré, and L. Van Langenhove (Eds.), *Rethinking methods in psychology* (pp. 9–26). London: SAGE.

Teske, P., & Schneider, M. (1999). *The importance of leadership: The role of school principals.* New York: The PricewaterhouseCoopers Endowment for the Business of Government.

Waters, T., & Grubb, S. (2004). *The leadership we need: Using research to strengthen the use of standards for administrator preparation and licensure programs.* Denver, CO: Mid-continent Research for Education and Learning.

Waters, T., Marzano, R., & McNulty, B. (2003). *Balanced leadership: What 30 years of research tells us about the effect of leadership on student achievement.* Aurora, CO: Mid-continent Research for Education and Learning.

Wendel, F. C., Hoke, F. A., & Joekel, R. G. (1996). *Outstanding school administrators: Their keys to success.* Westport, CO: Praeger.

Suggested Readings

- Buckingham, M., & Clifton, D. (2001). *Now, discover your strengths.* New York: The Free Press.

Using an online survey, readers identify five themes of individual strengths. Then, the authors show readers how to leverage the strengths for success as a manager of others.

- Collins, J. (2002). *Built to last*: *Successful habits of visionary companies.* New York: HarperCollins.

The prequel to *Good to Great,* this book covers the principles and practices of great companies, using a variety of companies that have lasted multiple chief officers for basis and comparisons.

- Collins, J. (2005). *Good to great and the social sectors*: *Why business thinking is not the answer,* Monograph to accompany *Good to great*: *Why some companies make the leap . . . and others don't* (Collins, 2001), Boulder, CO: Author.

Collins reacts to questions about application of findings in *Good to Great*: *Why Some Companies Make the Leap . . . and Others Don't* to the social sector. The monograph looks at measuring success, getting things done from a diffuse power structure, getting the right people on the bus, and rethinking the economic engine all from the perspective of the social sector.

- Downey, C. J. (2004). *The three-minute classroom walk-through*: *Changing supervisory practice one teacher at a time.* Thousand Oaks, CA: Corwin Press.

The author presents a curriculum-monitoring technique that capitalizes on building relationships through engaging teachers in reflective dialogue and focusing the energies of a school organization to enhance classroom instruction.

- Drucker, P. (2002). *The effective executive: The definitive guide to getting the right things done.* New York: HarperBusiness Essentials.

Drucker is the author of the 53-year-old management classic, *The Practice of Management.* In *The Effective Executive,* Drucker identifies five practices essential to business effectiveness that can—and must—be learned. He demonstrates the distinctive skill of the executive and offers fresh insights into old and seemingly obvious business situations.

- DuFour, R., Eaker, R., & DuFour, R. (Eds.). (2005). *On common ground: The power of professional learning communities.* Bloomington, IN: Solution Tree.

DuFour, Eaker, and DuFour offer a compendium of essays about the impact of collaboration and relationships in schools organized as professional learning communities.

- Frase, L., & Hetzel, R. (1990). *School management by wandering around.* Lanham, MD: Scarecrow Press.

This book offers specific strategies and techniques for using "management by wandering around" (MBWA) to obtain excellence in schools. It is a logical companion to the Downey book, *The Three-Minute Classroom Walk-Through,* described above.

- Frase, L., & Streshly, W. (2000). *The top 10 myths in education.* Lanham, MD: The Scarecrow Press.

The authors expose 10 of the common myths about American public schools—myths that have blocked meaningful school reform for decades. The book is a must read for educational policy makers and administrators.

- Fullan, M. (2001). *Leading in a culture of change.* San Francisco: Jossey-Bass.

Fullan draws on the most current ideas and theories of effective leadership, incorporating case studies to identify five core competencies of leadership.

- Kochanek, J. R. (2005). *Building trust for better schools*: *Research-based practices.* Thousand Oaks, CA: Corwin Press.

Besides making a case for the importance of trust, Kochanek offers an innovative process model of trust building in schools. Case studies of three schools are included.

- Kouzes, J. M., & Posner, B. Z. (2002). *The leadership challenge* (3rd ed.). San Francisco: Jossey-Bass.

The book describes five practices of exemplary leadership based on extensive research by the authors.

- Matsui, B. (2002). *The Ysleta story*: *A tipping point in education.* Claremont, CA: The Institute at Indian Hill/CGU.

The Ysleta Story is the inspiring tale of a school district that wasn't supposed to succeed—but did.

- McEwan, E. (2003). *10 traits of highly effective principals*: *From good to great performance.* Thousand Oaks, CA: Corwin Press.

This book provides principals, administrative teams, and educators with resources to hone 10 skills and traits of highly effective principals.

- Peters, T. J., & Waterman, R. H. (1982). *In search of excellence*: *Lessons from America's best-run companies.* Reprint (2004). New York: HarperBusiness Essentials.

Based on a study of 43 of America's best-run companies from a diverse array of business sectors. This book describes eight basic principles of management that made these organizations successful.

- Pfeffer, I., & Sutton, R. (2000). *The knowing-doing gap*: *How smart companies turn knowledge into action.* Boston: Harvard Business Press.

The authors break down the causes of the gap between our knowledge and the application of that knowledge in business into five main reasons. After backing-up each reason with facts and examples, direct solutions are given to its remedy. Eight guidelines for action are then presented. Case studies of businesses that have made huge turn-arounds using this approach are included.

- Sousa, D. A. (2003). *The leadership brain: How to lead today's schools more effectively.* Thousand Oaks, CA: Corwin Press.

The book examines what we know about the adult brain as applicable to leadership practice that sustains effective teaching and learning. The leadership practices described are compatible with Level 5 leadership.

- Streshly, W. A., Walsh, J., & Frase, L. E. (2002). *Avoiding legal hassles: What school administrators really need to know* (2nd ed.). Thousand Oaks, CA: Corwin Press.

A practical, nuts and bolts discussion of the school leader's role in the public school's conformance with school law—from the point of view of the practitioner. It is a practical guide to legally sound school planning.

- Waters, T., & Grubb, S. (2004). *The leadership we need.* Mid-continent Research for Education and Learning. Retrieved July 10, 2006, from http://www.mcrel.org

A gentle, but honest, critique of the ISLLC standards for training administrators by researchers from McREL—a must read for everyone connected with preparing school leaders. The document includes standards with supporting research gleaned from metaanalyses.

Index

CORWIN
PRESS

The Corwin Press logo—a raven striding across an open book—represents the union of courage and learning. Corwin Press is committed to improving education for all learners by publishing books and other professional development resources for those serving the field of PreK–12 education. By providing practical, hands-on materials, Corwin Press continues to carry out the promise of its motto: **Helping Educators Do Their Work Better.**

NATIONAL ASSOCIATION OF ELEMENTARY SCHOOL PRINCIPALS
Serving All Elementary and Middle Level Principals

The 29,500 members of the National Association of Elementary School Principals provide administrative and instructional leadership for public and private elementary and middle schools throughout the United States, Canada, and overseas. Founded in 1921, NAESP is today a vigorously independent professional association with its own headquarters building in Alexandria, Virginia, just across the Potomac River from the nation's capital. From this special vantage point, NAESP conveys the unique perspective of the elementary and middle school principal to the highest policy councils of our national government. Through national and regional meetings, award-winning publications, and joint efforts with its 50 state affiliates, NAESP is a strong advocate both for its members and for the 33 million American children enrolled in preschool, kindergarten, and Grades 1 through 8.